Sta...
...Bank

Didn't We Hope That It Wasn't Your Feet?
(A slow waltz)

Didn't we hope that it wasn't your feet
Sticking out under an olive-green sheet

Didn't we reason it wasn't your lark
You'd have driven not ridden round Florida Park

Hadn't we marvelled that you'd found the time
Not only to hold up but also to dine

Didn't we long not only for rain
But that you'd come back and rob us again

Waiting for rain. Waiting for hail
Hopes turn to ashes. Prints in the mail

Dust rain hail ashes – R I P
But the love of evil is the root of money
We try to be good but there're always some snags
And all our righteousnesses are as filthy rags

I don't know if a cyclone is better than drought
I don't know if Plet's in or if Plet is out
But I know that I hoped that it wasn't your feet
Sticking out under an olive-green sheet

Christopher Torr

Stander
...Bank Robber

Paul Moorcraft
Mike Cohen

GALAGO

JOHANNESBURG · LONDON

Dedicated to Letitia Snyman ... Miss South Africa 1984
... the one who also got away?

Books by Paul Moorcraft

A SHORT THOUSAND YEARS
CONTACT II
AFRICA'S SUPER POWER
CHIMURENGA
STANDER ... BANK ROBBER

Books by Mike Cohen

STANDER ... BANK ROBBER

© 1984 by Paul Moorcraft & Mike Cohen
All rights reserved

ISBN 0 947020 05 5

First published by Galago Publishing as
an original paperback, March 1984

Galago Books are published by
Galago Publishing (Pty) Ltd, P.O. Box 404, Alberton 1450, RSA
Tel: (011) 869-0807
and
Galago Publishing Ltd, 2nd Floor, Bromley Shopping Hall
16-20 Widmore Road, Kent, England
Tel: (01)460-2136

Type transferred electronically from
Galago computer setting by
Pictorial Process

Half tone reproductions by Pictorial Process

Printed by Printpak (Cape) Ltd

Book design and cover painting by Francis Lategan

Authors' Acknowledgements

To complete such a detailed enquiry as the writing of this book has entailed, we had to rely upon the support of a large number of people. Particular thanks are due to the Editor of the *Star,* Harvey Tyson, and the newspaper's crime reporter, Trevor Jones, also to the numerous members of the South African Police who assisted the authors, but particularly to Lieutenant General C.F. Zietsman, Brigadier F. Spies, Brigadier J. Fourie, Brigadier H. van der Linde, Brigadier W. van der Merwe, Major G. Viljoen, Captain L. Knipe and Captain F. Peach. The willing assistance of the Fort Lauderdale Police, Florida, is also acknowledged. Much hard work was done by the Directors and staff of Galago Publishing, particularly Peter Stiff who edited it, Francis Lategan who arted it and Amy Benecke for her dazzling work on the word processor.

Thanks too to Kitt Katzin, Mrs Boshoff at Beeld, Chris Steyn of the *Rand Daily Mail,* Dominique Gilbert of the *Sunday Times* who obtained and translated two letters written by André Stander.

Song, *Didn't We Hope That It Wasn't Your Feet?* reproduced by kind permission of Christopher Torr.

We would also like to thank the many people who let us interview them, often on very sensitive and grief stricken matters. And many colleagues on newspapers – the cartoonists, photographers, librarians and last but not least, those in the newsrooms – deserve our gratitude. Photographs are courtesy of the *Star, Sunday Express, Beeld, Rapport, Sunday Times* and *Associated Press.* Other pictures were taken by Marda de Wet (back cover) and Paul Moorcraft. Cartoon credits: Ken Smith (The *Star*), Louw Henning *(Rapport)* and Tony Grogan *(Cape Times)*

Bibliography

During the writing of this book accounts in the following newspapers were found helpful:

Argus, Cape Times, the *Star, Rand Daily Mail, Sunday Times, Sunday Express, Sunday Tribune, Rapport, Beeld, Pretoria News, Die Vaderland,* and the *Daily News.*

1

The Escape

11th August 1983

It was almost noon in Cullinan, a small town near Pretoria, the administrative capital of South Africa. Cullinan is a town with a diamond mine; without the diamond mine there wouldn't be a town. The most magnificent segment of the renowned Cullinan diamond is set in Queen Elizabeth's royal crown.

It looked as if it was going to be just another uneventful day in an always uneventful dorp. Throughout the dry provinces of South Africa the savage drought dragged on, as did that day in Cullinan.

A local physiotherapist, Mrs Amelia Grobler, had had a busy morning. Her waiting room was full. She was expecting several hard labour prisoners from Zonderwater maximum security prison, which is in the locality of Cullinan.

Amelia Grobler attended to all the prison's physiotherapy needs but, unknown to her, that day was to become probably the most memorable one of her life.

It was the first time she had been called upon to deal with prisoners of the calibre of hardness that typified André Charles Stander and Patrick Leigh McCall, known to his friends and family as Leigh, both long term prisoners being escorted to her rooms for treatment.

Within a few minutes of their arrival together with their prison guard escorts at her rooms, events would occur which would trigger off a saga of crime that would capture the imagination of the whole country.

South Africa would soon eagerly await the daily news of their exploits, particularly of the leader, André Stander.

Yet, in little more than five months, both Stander and McCall would have been shot to death. So even on that quiet day in Cullinan when all the excitement was about to break, there was only a little of the sands of time left for each of them.

Stander, the former police captain turned villain, was to be transformed into a folk hero by many South Africans.

People clearly prefer to worship anti-authoritarian heroes, like Scotty Smith, Billy the Kid or Ned Kelly, even if they are good bad men or bad good men. In fact, in time, their criminal foibles and inclinations are forgiven and only their daring is remembered.

Stander, the son of a retired police general, was serving a prison sentence of seventy five years in hard labour, of which period, because of sentences running concurrently, he would have to serve an effective seventeen and a half years for bank holdups.

A Man's Man

He was a man's man and a woman's man as well, ruggedly tough, bright perhaps but very complex in his personality.

André Stander hated prison in the way that only a man who had once served on the more respectable side of the law could hate it. Only days before his appointment with the physiotherapist he had written to his father, retired South African Police General Frans Stander, pleading with him to do something to get him out of gaol.

Stander had only made two real friends in prison, his cell mate Patrick Leigh McCall who had been declared an habitual criminal for car thefts and fraud, and another convict serving time for bank robberies, the very intelligent Allan George Heyl. Stander and McCall had become naturally

8

friendly – having been forced to spend so much time in each other's company during their confinement. Heyl, apparently, had stayed in the background, probably because the convicts had not wanted to be seen spending too much time together, in case it aroused suspicions of an impending escape bid.

On the day of their appointment with Mrs Amelia Grobler Heyl had stayed behind in his cell in the concrete and iron complex of the Zonderwater Prison.

Stander and McCall, together with five other long term prisoners in need of treatment, had been escorted to Cullinan by three of the regular prison warders.

The symptoms of injury necessitating their appointments, made through the Prison authorities by Stander and McCall, had been faked as a part of a well organised and carefully thought out escape plan.

The stocky, one meter eighty two centimeter, eighty kilogram Stander and the slightly built and shorter McCall were well behaved model prisoners.

The seven prisoners were brought into Mrs Grobler's rooms by the warders and ordered to sit down in the waiting room to bide their time.

Midday Break-Out

Shortly before midday Stander and McCall suddenly leapt up.

After a short but violent struggle they overpowered their unsuspecting guards. Because they had gained the element of surprise, the struggle didn't last long and both convicts were quickly armed with their former captors' service pistols.

While all this had been going on the other five prisoners had stood aside, refusing to take part in the break out.

The physiotherapist, Mrs Grobler, unsuspectingly entered the waiting room from her office. The two escapees immediately confronted her and threatened to shoot her. She had no option but to hand them her car keys.

The keys, of course, were to be their ticket to freedom.

They jumped into the car and Stander gunned it in the direction of Tembisa, a black township; an area which was familiar territory for Stander who had been stationed there for several years as a policeman. He had also had been engaged on riot duty there during the 1976 unrest in the black locations.

The men's future actions were now fraught with hazard. Either they had to burrow down into immediate hiding, or they had to assume different identities to put the forces of law and order off their scent.

They were still wearing prison garb, something which was sure to be noted by anyone who saw them.

By this time, of course, the escape had been reported to the Police and a massive manhunt for them had been mounted.

Only seven kilometers away from Cullinan, Stander decided to turn off and follow a dirt road. Eventually, in the Rayton district, the fugitives came upon the farm of forty eight year old Martin Riekert who lived there with his wife and eighteen year old son, Henk. The men of the farm were at home, working in the farmyard, when the stolen car driven by the fugitives turned into the access road of their property.

Farmer Riekert approached the car as it stopped in the drive by the farmhouse. He gulped in shock as he found himself staring down the barrel of a pistol. Henk Riekert strolled across to the car to see what was going on and in moments he too found himself held up by the two wanted men.

Brazen Exploit

A brazen exploit indeed – but brazen was to be the hallmark of the Stander gang's future exploits.

Stander told Riekert to telephone the local police and get them around to the farm on some pretext.

Once done, they all sat down in the farmhouse to await their arrival.

Stander and his colleagues kept their guns ready to use, and soon captured the young constable who pitched up at the farmhouse to investigate Riekert's alleged complaint.

Things were going much better than they had expected.

The policeman, Constable Mossie Mostert, was well

known to the Riekert family. He had been stationed in the area for some time and was known to most of the locals, and he certainly had not expected the reception he got.

Stander and McCall added Mossie Mostert's pistol to their armaments.

Mr Riekert, his son, and Constable Mostert were bundled into the cage of the van and locked in. They did not resist, for the escapers were armed and seemed ready to open fire in case of resistance.

The escaped convicts, together with their prisoners, then continued their drive towards Tembisa.

On their way another plan emerged. It was clear the escapees had to lay their hands on a civilian car. A car that would not be subject to immediate recognition, such as a police car. They stopped the van and Stander got out. McCall got into the driver's seat and drove the police vehicle into a secluded side road.

Their new plan involved making themselves appear as official and above board as possible.

Meanwhile, twenty seven year old Nakkie Fouche, a nurse employed at Tembisa hospital, was driving to work shortly before 3.00 pm. Although not late for work, she was nevertheless driving her vehicle at a good speed.

Suddenly, a policeman stepped into the road and flagged her down. He was wearing a uniform and she did not doubt his bona fides.

Not wanting to evade the law Mrs Fouche stopped her car, a silver grey Opel, to see what he wanted, suspecting all the time that she had been caught exceeding the speed limit.

Mrs Fouche was immediately dragged from her car and hustled into the police van. It was an arrest but, whatever it was that she had done, she knew she had done nothing to deserve treatment like that.

André Stander, for he was the man in uniform, unceremoniously shoved her into the cage of the van, to join his three other captives.

The criminals now possessed an unidentified getaway car.

McCall got behind the wheel of the Opel, while Stander drove in front with the police truck. They then travelled for a number of kilometers before stopping.

They were now ready to go it alone, and they drove off in the Opel leaving their captives behind, still locked in the police van.

Beginning of an Arsenal

They had gathered up four guns by this time, but this number would soon grow into a veritable arsenal.

Constable Mossie Mostert, helped by Henk Riekert, managed to get free of the van. They achieved this by kicking out the small window between the cage and the cab.

Once free they walked to the nearest police station and reported what had happened.

But, during the time it had taken them to get help, Stander and McCall had managed to get clear, evading the massive police dragnet which had been put out. For a while they had simply disappeared.

The Police were not happy that the men they had taken so much trouble to catch had escaped so easily from prison.

They described both wanted men as extremely dangerous.

The four kidnap victims were shocked but unharmed. They had been threatened with firearms, which they had all thought the escapers would not hesitate to use, but had not been assaulted or roughed up. This was to become, on the surface at least, an apparent style and Stander was even, sometimes, described as gentlemanly. But even in England, once upon a time, highwaymen were euphemistically called 'gentlemen of the road' but they were still hanged on gibbets at Tyburn Hill.

The Police were not fooled and the public were repeatedly warned of their dangerous traits in the Press and on radio and TV and advised to avoid contact with the two fugitives.

Stander, who was very concerned about his mother, telephoned a woman at Boksburg who later told the Police. He asked her to ring his mother in Pretoria and tell her he was not hurt and everything was okay.

The car stolen from Mrs Nakkie Fouche was later found in the Tembisa location.

For the next six months Stander's exploits were to make headlines. His audacity and apparent ability to outfox the Police, who were determinedly hunting him, turned the tough cop into a folk hero, despite the constant growling condemnation of newspaper editorials.

His crimes and hints of high living between escapades enthralled the public, only too ready to enjoy a local, real life soap opera.

'Anyway, whatever you say about him he hasn't killed anyone,' was the parrot cry.

Death Wish

Underneath the bravado and cunning, however, many people sensed that Stander had a death wish. Lieutenant General Christie Zietsman, who commanded the police hunt for Stander, said: 'It's just a matter of time. It can only finish in one way. It's like a Greek tragedy. The end is inevitable.'

The Police privately admitted that they felt it unlikely they would take him alive and they didn't. Then, when he was killed and while the South African Police breathed a collective sigh of relief that the hunt was over, many thousands of South Africans mourned that the big chase had finally ended in a shootout in which Stander had died and that he didn't get away after all.

And so a legend was born. Graffiti appeared on walls.

'Stander Lives' slogans proclaimed.

In this way André Stander joined the Che Guevaras of this world in the list of popular although tainted saints.

How did this former policeman, who turned to crime and broke his father's heart, win the admiration and affection of so many South Africans?

Where did it all start?

2

Greek Tragedy

General Zietsman was right: the Stander saga had contained all the elements of a Greek tragedy. But what was it that drove André Stander to his perhaps inevitable doom?

It seemed logical that young André would one day join the Police. His father, Frans, was a highly successful career officer who finally, after the best part of fifty years of unblemished service, reached the rank of general before retirement. His job, as is inevitable with a career policeman, took him to many stations and posts around the country and because of this André had to change schools many times.

At the end of it all he failed a number of exams and finally his matric.

But his school friend, Hennie van der Merwe, confirmed that he was bright. Although André didn't excel he never used to study. In fact, as far as Hennie remembered, Stander never opened a book outside of school.

Bob Dylan

But André grew very fond of poetry, especially the works of Bob Dylan. Secretly, his close friends say, he used to compose verse himself. Hennie van der Merwe remarked that André Stander was not at all well behaved.

'He was naughty like other boys. He stole small things.'

Another schoolfriend, however, says Stander once stole his father's official police car and took it for a joyride which can hardly be classified as just naughty.

It was perhaps his son's educational failures and way-wardness that encouraged the general to push his son to-wards a career in the South African Police. Apparently his actions soon paid off. André was adjudged the best recruit in his intake into the Pretoria Police College in 1964. He worked his way rapidly through the ranks, attaining his commission and joining the Criminal Investigation Department. In his early thirties he became the detachment commander at Kempton Park. At the time of his arrest he was CID detachment commander at Boksburg, pending a transfer to Evander.

He had everything going for him in the South African Police, although some senior officers have described him as ecame South Africa's most wanted criminal.

Why?

Stander had a complex personality. Maybe, like the Jekylls and Hydes of this world, he had many personalities. The more one talks to his friends and associates, the more his personal mystery deepens. He has been variously described as intelligent, as fashion conscious, as a fitness fanatic, as an outdoors man, as an expert on food and wine, as a deep thinker, as a poet, as an animal lover, that he was introverted, shy, likeable and kind as well.

Excellent Taste

One girl friend, Carol van der Merwe, said: 'He knew how to treat people. He gave beautiful presents. He had excellent taste.'

Another girl friend, Sue Hewitt, said he was 'a perfect gentleman, any girl's dream man'.

But, if he was all these things, why did such a perfect gentleman become the leader of a mob as ruthless as the Stander gang?

His father, Frans Stander, always stood by his son. His belief is that three events changed his son's life. First was the haunting memories of the 1976 disturbances in which André Stander alleges he killed twenty two rioters in Tembisa township. André Stander used the term 'blood baths' when describing events there. (It must be said that these alleged shootings by Stander have doubtful standing.)

Entire Personality Change

After that experience, according to his father, 'André had an entire personality change'.

'I regretted that I had influenced him to become a policeman because it was not initially his intention. He would not have been involved in these shootings had he not been a policeman.'

The second incident was the death of his brother, Brian, who was killed in a train accident in 1978. André had been close to his brother.

Brian Stander was the younger of the two brothers, only fifteen months separating them. They grew up as if they were twins. Brian was an outstanding sportsman and André hero worshipped him.

The younger Stander was an assistant train driver with the South African Railways. On 28th January 1978 there was a terrible storm near Brits, west of Pretoria. Brian was on a locomotive en route to Pretoria station when a railway bridge was washed away by the driving rain. The locomotive left the line and fell into a deep culvert. Brian was killed, apparently almost instantly.

André was formally asked to attend at the mortuary to identify the body before the post mortem. 'This should never have happened,' his father said. He became hysterical because the body was so badly mutilated.

The third incident to affect his personality was the divorce from his wife Leonie, to whom he gave the pet name of Bekkie.

Later when André Stander was arrested, and afterwards when the family fought for a retrial, the alleged Tembisa incidents and the rogue cop's relations with his wife were extensively discussed.

Tembisa

In Stander's own words during his trial for robbery: 'I went to Tembisa with high regard for the Police Force, crime combat and the general police treatment of black people

'To say my world collapsed there is perhaps put dramatically, but my blinkers were certainly removed there.

'The confusion and chaos that reigned there, the unlimited hysteria which experienced police officers denied existed, was for me the most unpleasant revelation and shock of my life.

'Black people who were mere spectators were outlawed and shot, it seemed to me.

'Everyone was shooting and hitting, and allowing dogs to rip human beings to pieces. Blood flowed everywhere . . . most of the corpses were removed by the inhabitants of Tembisa and the real death count was much higher than was officially furnished.

'The scene at the Tembisa police station back yard reminded me of scenes one saw of wars. It was blood and corpses; at times wounded people who lay groaning received only curses in reply to their complaints and request for treatment.

'My already tottering confidence completely cracked. I was in a state of permanent shock and my nerves were shot.'

Of course, at this time Stander was fighting for his life and anything in mitigation he could find to diminish the possibility that he would be sentenced to death for armed robbery was vital.

However, it seems reasonable to suppose that if his nerves were shot by his Tembisa experiences, then he soon recovered, for the ice cool nerves he displayed during the course of his bank robberies certainly didn't indicate a man on the brink of nervous collapse. Neither did it indicate that the use of guns in anger had brought about a repugnance for their use.

Relations With His Wife

Besides Tembisa, his relations with his wife influenced Stander. In a statement made on the 23rd August 1982, which was later handed to the court, his ex-wife explained:

'André's job was his life and he forgot about me. Sometimes he wouldn't come home for two weeks.'

Leonie and André met in 1967, and got married in 1969. Two years later they were divorced. But they remarried in

1975.

'After a few weeks André was sent for three months anti-terrorist training at Groblersdal,' she said.

'With his return he said he was so ready for slaughter after everything he'd learned and found out during training that he could almost lay his hands on any black he found in the streets.

'When a tap was left dripping, he became furiously angry and immediately stormed at the tap, closing it and then blamed me for it, resulting in hefty arguments.

'He was abrupt with me and forced me to learn how to describe people, to memorise car registration numbers, etc.

'Shortly afterwards the unrest in Tembisa began. One day after work I found a letter on my bed with a pistol next to it. The safety catch was off and he explained he was scared that blacks would want to harm me because he was with the police. After a long night during the dreadful unrests, André came home and sat on the ground against the wall and quietly tried to explain how he felt.

'He mentioned that at one moment there would be nothing and literally the next moment you would be powerless and can you shoot or can't you shoot, but also do you want to shoot or not. The feeling of stones on your car . . . and then the faces of wounded people who collapsed before you – wounded or dead; men, women and children, many of them innocent.

'Then a few hours later when they had to count the corpses, you realise there should be a few more dead – but that these people removed the corpses before the police could get there.

'André obviously became withdrawn. Every morning he went running alone with his dogs; he became engrossed in his music and our personal contact was minimal.'

He loved his eight dogs very much, especially Shalom. But he mistreated Shalom so atrociously when he was cross that she had to stop him.

'Once he lifted Shalom above his head and with all his strength threw him on the ground, jumped on the dog with both feet and all his weight.

'When I stopped him he quietened down and walked away and later when I saw him again, he lay on the ground with his hands around Shalom, tears in his eyes and kissed the dog all over his body. He was never violent with me, but took it out on the dog. He wanted to own me but without taking responsibility.'

Leonie must have loved Stander very much to endure such strains. Eventually she walked out on him in 1978 and finally divorced him in February 1979.

There were no children.

These pressures, according to his family and his ex-wife, made him resent the Police.

Rejection of Authority

According to General Frans Stander, his son's rejection of authority problems began in 1971. In an application to the Durban Supreme Court for a retrial for his son in October 1982 he claimed that 'the judge had erred by emphasising the interests of the community and had not paid enough attention to André Stander's circumstances.'

In 1969 General Stander was the Divisional Criminal Investigation Department Officer for the Northern Transvaal. He asked his son to form a unit to fight the sharp increase of drugs on the Rand.

'He excelled himself so that he was in great demand throughout the country for help and advice . . . he gave lectures to the public and schools about drugs. He flourished in this type of work.

'I believe,' the general continued, 'that André's problems started when I was transferred to the West Rand as Divisional Criminal Investigation Officer in 1971.

'My successor did not like my methods. He brought changes which restricted the freedom of others. André was unhappy with this change. He and his men believed that everything they had worked such long hours for had been lost. He began to lose interest in the Police as a career.'

Whether this is, in fact, true and whether the school which suggests that his new, perhaps more conservative, commander disapproved of Stander's Al Pacino style of detective approach of wearing long hair and fashionable clothes to make merging with the criminal element easier, or whether it was more that his abilities as a policeman did not measure up so well once he was away from the protected environment created by his father being his officer commanding, must cause some mature thought. But whatever it was and whatever the reason, Stander was transferred away from the Division to Kokstad in the Free State.

So far as his father's views are concerned, it is not unknown in disciplined forces for old commanders to growl disapproval at their successor's new broom and different methods of running their commands.

The policeman closest to him in Kokstad, now a senior non-commissioned officer serving in Durban, said: 'André Stander was a common criminal but still a great guy.

'I think he had his differences with the Police Force. He couldn't take the red tape. Yet, he was a good policeman and a very intelligent guy. I lost touch with him after his promotion to the rank of lieutenant.'

As part of Stander's career he was sent on a counter-insurgency course at Malooskop near Groblersdal, in the Eastern Transvaal, in 1975. This course, too, had a negative effect on him, according to his father.

Burden of Frustration?

From the family's perspective, the brilliant cop became transformed under the burden of his frustration with the Police, his personal tragedies and his failed marriage.

His mother testified in mitigation at his trial. 'If André is guilty of all the things they say he is, he must have gone mad.' She also said: 'I think he had had a nervous breakdown.'

But the sudden transformation, the nervous breakdown theory, can be questioned. His record at school was troublesome, not brilliant. At one time during the hunt for the Stander gang, former police colleague Chris Swanepoel said: 'You know, we read every day of the brilliant student who was forced on the road to robbery. Brilliant? How could he be brilliant and still fail matric? Oh sure, he was a captain in the Police but was he a brilliant detective? Rubbish I say. When we were in the Force together he couldn't even catch a cold.'

He was reputed to love animals but his former wife, Bekkie, tells how in a fit of temper he once threw a pet dog of theirs to the ground and stamped on it. Hardly the behaviour of an animal lover.

Perhaps his personality contradictions had always been embedded in Stander's psyche. A man who when at school never read a book but who later, according to a long standing woman friend, 'practically devoured books and literature, but always of the kind where there was a super type hero into whose shoes he could project himself.'

One Woman – the Cause?

He disliked authority yet he joined the Police Force. Perhaps hidden inside the cop was someone who really wanted to be a suave, chic, jet-set type hero. Stander's one time schoolfriend, Hennie van der Merwe, was asked why he thought Stander turned from keeping the law to breaking the law. 'So far as I am concerned Bekkie came from a well to do family. She's really a wonderful person, but at times a bit demanding. André always wanted to prove to her that one day he would be a rich man as well. That, so far as I'm concerned, was the main factor that pushed him on the road to crime.

'He was always trying to prove to her that he could provide her with the good things in life. He wanted to buy a boat . . . a bigger than normal swimming pool.'

Louis Kruger, the man who served under Stander at the Criminal Investigation Department Kempton Park, said: 'Bekkie was just a normal sort of person really. But she had a very highly paid job of her own. I think he found it difficult to keep up with her.'

But Cor van Deventer, the former policeman and Bureau for State Security official who informed on his best friend Stander, disagrees.

'Was one woman the cause of Stander's downfall?' asked Van Deventer.

'That's bullshit. When she married him she knew he was just a poor policeman. There cannot be a girl in South

Africa who believes the South African Police is a Force of millionaires. If she really wanted more out of life she wouldn't have married the guy. She always did the cooking and the housework. She was quite content sitting around her home, not going out and not spending money. I cannot remember one occasion where she ever demanded that he take her out to dinner. Never. I always thought she was happy with very little and with the simple life.'

Van Deventer also rejected the theory that the Tembisa riots affected Stander.

'No, I don't accept that. He was supposed to have shot twenty two people, but I never heard about it.

Don't you think he would have told his best friend about it some time or another if it really happened?'

But the former South African Police lieutenant, Louis Kruger, a man who worked very closely with Stander during the 1976 riots, had a different view on the allegation that Stander had killed twenty two people at Tembisa while helping to quell the riots and disturbances there. An allegation, incidentally, that the South African Police denies.

Drag Bodies Away

'During riots in African locations, it often happens that people are shot and killed by police and then deaths never find their way into the official police figures. This is not because the Police falsify body counts, but because friends and relatives drag bodies away for burial before they can be recovered and taken to the mortuary,' Louis Kruger said.

This argument is, of course, highly plausible for a number of reasons – fear of police reprisals, personal factors – there have been many known examples of relatives removing bodies before the authorities could get hold of them, sometimes even from mortuaries.

Kruger continued: 'I helped in the investigations of the sudden death dockets for inquest purposes. In many instances there is the possibility that more deaths arose than was known. It is quite possible in my belief that this squad was responsible for twenty deaths.

'André was one of the very few really honest men at those riots. A lot of men probably did things they should not have done during that period, yet André, I know, stepped forward and said that he had given the order to open fire. Some of the others weren't quite so open.

'I think it caused him to lose interest in the Police Force and in continuing to be a policeman. He began palming most of the work off on to me, as I was his second in charge. He could have done better, but he was one of the best the Police Force had.'

Nevertheless, if Kruger's contention that Stander could have killed or been responsible for the deaths of twenty African rioters is correct, it still seems strange that all – or just about all – the bodies disappeared. After all, not every rioter takes friends and relatives with him to a riot.

Stander was a man of contradictions who stimulated contradictory responses, even in his closest friends, and of that there is no doubt.

His parents were both dedicated to him, and the father-son bond always seemed strong.

Louis Kruger spoke of Stander's family relations.

'André always got on well with his father. He once said that he thought his mother was sometimes a little bit high and mighty. She was certainly a very sophisticated lady and he wished she wasn't always like that.'

But Cor van Deventer, perhaps the man who knew Stander best before he went to gaol, says that 'he never really talked with a lot of respect about his parents'.

Yet his distraught but proud father always fought long and hard to protect his son, blaming his crimes and derelictions on the deterioration of his son's psychological condition.

Other evidence, however, suggests that the 'brilliant cop turned crook' description is very wide of the mark, that it is more likely he was always bent.

Stander had walked on the wild side of life long before the events of 1976.

In 1968 he arrested a drug dealer in Durban. The dealer has told the authors that Stander said he wouldn't turn him in if he gave information about someone else; which he did. This in itself, it is stressed, is not unusual in the *quid pro quo* game of police underworld dealings.

He afterwards became a friend of Stander and says: 'on one occasion he even warned me that other policemen were about to bust me.'

Another time, after discussing 'how my first trip (on acid) affected me,' Stander said: 'The police need a sample. Can you get me one?'

It was tacitly understood between them that Stander was about to experiment.

'Was Stander born bad?' Van Deventer was asked.

He paused and thought before answering.

'Some people,' he said ' are born black and some are born white. But I don't think anybody is born bad.'

Actions not Opinions

Perhaps the actions of Stander – not the opinions of friends, enemies and family – should speak for themselves. His criminal career was unique, not just his *modus operandi* and pluck, but also his motivation.

After his prison escape, a retired former Murder and Robbery Squad captain, Jack le Grange, spoke about Stander.

'Most escaped prisoners try to disappear, to get away, but Stander is different. He's going nowhere because he has a self imposed mission to fulfill. He's got a horrible grudge.'

Was it a grudge against himself, his family, the South African Police or society as a whole?

The grudge, whatever it was and whatever caused it, worked its way to the surface in 1977 when Stander was commanding the Criminal Investigation Department detachment at Kempton Park Police station.

It was there that he developed his criminal master plan. It was simple, unorthodox and even brilliant. It was designed to beat society but, finally, in the drizzling rain on a Fort Lauderdale street in the United States of America, society beat him.

3

Captain Jekyll and Robber Hyde

1977-1979

Stander became a classic Jekyll and Hyde. Openly to his friends and police colleagues he was a successful policeman. In reality he had changed into a successful crook.

In just under three years from 1977 until his arrest in 1980 he hit a string of banks in Durban and on the Rand, netting himself at least one hundred thousand rand.

His *modus operandi* was to catch an early morning flight to Durban from Jan Smuts Airport and arrive there before 9.00 am. Once there he would don the disguise of his choice for the day, hire or steal a car and then set out for his first target.

His criminal efforts gained him the nickname of the 'gentleman robber', because he was always polite when he held people up with a gun.

Ruthless Edge

But Captain Stander's tactics had a hard and ruthless edge. As Duncan Williams, a teller in the Umhlanga Rocks branch of Barclays Bank that Stander held up on 12th November 1979, said: 'A fairly tall man came up to me, told me it was a robbery and said I was to hand over the money in the till. He had a gun and he told me not to try anything funny. He said he had already shot a person earlier that day and he didn't want to do it again.'

It might have been a bluff, but Williams was not in a position to know that. In any case, loaded guns – and Stander always carried loaded guns – are not for decoration.

As a solo robber, the larger banking establishments and building societies were out of his reach. Instead, he concentrated on places where there were only a few employees on whom he could easily keep an eye.

A few hours after each robbery Stander would catch an aircraft and fly back to Jan Smuts.

Meanwhile, back at his station, the commander of the Criminal Investigation Department – Captain Stander - would always be 'out on an investigation', or simply 'away for the day'.

Sometimes Stander would leave his office only for a few hours and tackle banks or building societies nearer his home base.

It all seemed so easy. So cool. But could it last?

Stander's former second in command at Kempton Park, Louis Kruger, said: 'While we were in the Force together, André used to disappear to Durban, telling me as his number two that he was going to buy or check on the curio shop stock (which he jointly owned – against police regulations – with Cor van Deventer). They were normal explanations every time. As far as I remember, he only travelled to Durban about five times at the most.

'He always told me to take the chair. He didn't have to give an explanation about his movements.'

During the period of his crime spree Stander's salary as a police officer increased from four hundred and eighty five rand to six hundred and eighty five rand – supplemented very much by his bank jobs.

'Jumping Jack'

Colonel Basie Smit, a results policeman known to the underworld as 'Jumping Jack', gave evidence of investigations he had carried out to find out what Stander had done with the R97 000 he had stolen during his two and a half year robbery spree.

He testified that Stander's house had been renovated

and that there was a new pool. There was a carport for four vehicles, a caravan and a trailer, a Ford Pirana car as well as another vehicle. Inside, the house had a well stocked built-in bar, four fridges and a room half filled with three thousand rands' worth of dried biltong. It was clear to Colonel Basie Smith at that time that Stander had handled at least R80 000, but he could only account for R47 000.

When asked what he had done with all the money Stander told the Colonel that he had wasted it.

During this time André Stander was generous to a fault with bank money he had stolen and lent over R16 000 to his friends.

A friend said: 'He would lend his buddies money and say "When you can return it, return it."'

Louis Kruger said: 'Maybe I am biased. He was a great friend. He was never selfish. He didn't skimp on money. Whenever we went for dinner he always paid. We were lieutenants together, then he was promoted above me to the rank of captain.'

Ian Odendaal and Boet van Heerden of Vryheid each revealed after his escape that they had both been good friends of Stander before his robbery convictions.

They recalled how he had won his colours for Eastern Transvaal at the tug o' war and mentioned the time he went to Swaziland with them to play rugby.

Odendaal was amazed at the amount of money, considering he was a salaried policeman, Stander gambled away in the casino. He was also staggered when he went to Stander's house and saw the luxury there – everything was push-button controlled.

Both men, however, unlike a lot of other friends and relatives, said they wouldn't have hesitated to hand him over to the Police had he contacted them when he was on the run.

Stander's extravagant life style aroused the curiosity of his police colleagues as well. Kruger explained that during this time Stander said he had inherited money from his father. His father told Stander that he should have it while he needed it and not have to wait for it until he died. That was the way he explained how he had managed to make such expensive improvements to his home.

The Curio Shop

Meanwhile, Stander had gone into business with his best friend, Cor van Deventer. They shared interests in the Zuza curio shop in Durban.

Stander had previously approached Kruger. 'André wanted me to go into the business with him. I refused. I think he finally held it against me.

'He eventually went into business with Cor van Deventer and a woman named Evelyn Schneider . . . the three of them kept the business going.'

Cor van Deventer testified during Stander's trial in 1980 that he had been asked by Stander to join him and Kruger in the formation of a bank robbery gang. Kruger, however, maintained that his friend only asked him to join him in the curio business.

Kruger resigned and left the South African Police after Stander was charged in 1980.

Bragging Led to Downfall

Finally, it was Stander's boasting that brought about his downfall.

He bragged to Van Deventer, that he had already hit over forty banks and building societies.

Initially, according to his testimony at the trial, Van Deventer did not take his friend seriously. As he put it himself: 'He teased me about my part time hawking to supplement my salary . . . I didn't believe what he said at all.'

But André began to tell him more and more. Even about his feelings when he robbed banks. 'He admitted to me,' said Van Deventer, 'that the first few times were sheer agony. He nearly dirtied his pants. But after that he couldn't stop. He began to enjoy himself. He used to watch the expressions on the faces of his victims. He was laughing up his sleeve as he committed his robberies. There was an element of sadistic bullying about it.

'He told me of one occasion when a teller in a building society gave him only about three hundred rand. He asked for more and the woman, who was greatly upset, emptied out her till to show that she didn't have any. "How do you expect me to live on this?" he said. Afterwards, when telling me about it, he couldn't stop laughing.'

Then the friendship broke down. Stander accused Van Deventer of stealing R7 000, the proceeds of one of his heists. 'For close on ten years he had been the best friend one could ever want,' Van Deventer said.

'When he started with this thing he changed towards me. He became a stranger.'

Colonel Basie Smit also gave evidence that there had been trouble between Cor van Deventer and Stander about money in their business, the Zuza curio shop.

When R7 000 of the money which Stander had allegedly stolen was restolen from the Maharani Hotel – into which he had booked under an assumed name – he accused Van Deventer of stealing it.

Colonel Smit said he found that the money had been stolen (but not by whom).

Relations with his wife, Bekkie, were also deteriorating. Affection for his dogs began to replace the human love he was missing.

'His dogs,' said Van Deventer, 'were trusted friends who could not talk back, who needed him as he needed them, in place of the children the marriage never produced.'

Arrest at Jan Smuts

Eventually Van Deventer made the decision to tell the Police what Stander had been up to and he contacted Colonel Basie Smit who was then commanding the South African Police Narcotics Bureau in Pretoria.

He gave Colonel Smit the keys to a white Toyota which Stander had allegedly stolen from Budget Car Hire at Louis Botha Airport in August 1979, and went with him to Jan Smuts Airport where he indicated the car which was in a bay in the undercover parking.

Colonel Smit opened the car and in the glove compartment he found, wrapped in a balaclava helmet, false wigs, a false beard, a false moustache, a bushscarf of the police issue type and a summons served on a Mr S J van Staden-Benade for exceeding the speed limit.

In the boot he found a false number plate and a roll of masking tape.

It was a tough decision for a tough cop. He had evidence that Stander was a crook, enough probably to convict him.

Should he grab him before he robbed again and perhaps killed someone, even though it would mean gaining conclusive evidence if he let him carry on to Durban. But what then if he returned by a different route or even slipped away into Swaziland.

Whatever the merits of the argument Colonel Smit took the tough decision.

He photographed everything, put them back where he had found them and relocked the car.

'The car was kept under observation,' said Colonel Smit, 'and on 2nd January I saw Mr Stander drive to Jan Smuts in a red Ford.'

He then took up position in the restaurant near the departure lounge and watched Stander board a Durban bound flight.

Meanwhile, a black constable who had been keeping observation on the white Toyota reported that Stander had opened it and removed certain items on his way to the departure lounge.

Colonel Smit then rechecked the car and ascertained that the balaclava helmet and its contents were missing.

The next day, the 3rd January, he received a report that Barclays Bank Durban North had been robbed of more than R4 940.

A Police General Was There Too

Observations on incoming Durban flights were mounted and on the 4th January, in the presence of Major General Kobus Visser, who then commanded the Criminal Investigation Department in South Africa, and other policemen, he arrested Stander as he entered the arrivals hall.

He was wearing dark glasses and carrying a case and a denim bag.

In his pocket he found a boarding ticket under the name of Mr D Johnson and his luggage labels matched this name. He also found a Book of Life issued to a Mr S J van Staden-

Benade with Stander's photograph glued on top of the original. There were also several bank books showing that various sums of money had been deposited in Stander's name.

They went to where the white Toyota was parked and a key found in Stander's pocket opened it.

They searched his luggage discovering cash to the value of R4 915, a balaclava, a .38 revolver, a false beard and a moustache.

Stander was clearly frightened and was sweating heavily. He refused to answer any questions but nodded when asked if the money was his.

Later, when Colonel Smit and Stander had a cup of coffee from Colonel Smit's flask, Stander 'appeared more relaxed'.

Stander then asked Smit to use some of the money to feed his dogs.

Smit was straightforward about what was clearly a spectacular case.

'To me the fact that he was a general's son made not the slightest difference. I investigated the case as I would any other, as I would indeed if it had been a Cabinet Minister, a high official or anybody else.'

The Double Life

There was little sympathy for the predicament Stander had found himself in from his former police colleagues on the East Rand.

They felt he deserved every bit of the sentence he eventually got. 'We do not feel in the least bit sorry for him,' one of them said. Another said: 'He should never have done what he did, In fact, he is still lucky to have got the sentence he did.'

Another who had been a close friend and who had worked alongside him said he was a good detective who worked long hours and who stood behind his men in trouble – but he should have known better.

'The news of his secret double life came as a terrible shock,' he continued. 'The worst thought is that he could have shot one of us in his escapades.'

General Frans Stander was bitter about the circumstances of his son's arrest. 'I retired,' he said, 'with an un-blemished record and they did not even have the decency to inform me first that my son was arrested for robbery. The first my wife and I heard about it was on the television.'

A Letter to His Parents

In a letter to his parents (a translated version of which appeared in the *Sunday Tribune*) Stander said:

Mum and Dad,

Maybe something has happened so that I can tell you both what people usually tell their parents when they are not there anymore. Namely, thank you Dad and Mum. I have not cried since the whole story began but I am now very close to it. With the thank you I also want to say sorry for the shame, the sorrow and everything this foolishness caused you.

I was surely half bevoetered in my head and things that made other people happy usually bored me. It would have been so much better and easier had I been like Flippie or someone like that hey, but I am not.

Everything happens for a reason and the big story here is that I admit I lost God years ago. I stopped praying, denied everything that is sacred and beautiful and simply just lived or existed.

I think you have recognised that I became a loner and was satisfied with nothing. I though I was looking for happiness but just had to look up and everything would have been there.

Sometimes I got near it through Holpsie recently and with Piet Laubser. I tried hard but since school days I've been a fool who couldn't learn the easy way.

No, my head works in completely the other way. I think it is a type of relationship one can describe this way: everyone goes one way, something which everyone can see can't be so wonderful, so I go the other way.

Maybe I see things differently and better than they do which makes me even more otherwise than all the rest of them.

Anyway, I love you both very much; thank you for all the trouble, love, loyalty and sorrow from '46 when I was born till now. I wish I could repay it but I can't. Just look how I've repaid it, with the biggest sorrow ever.

I am so sorry, but a good thing is that it is a wonderful thing God has now given me a chance and I took it. I was too big for my shoes, now I am an ant again.

I want to promise you that never will I be the same person again. I looked for trouble and walked into it with open eyes. I blame nobody, I believe it was God's will to bring me back to Him.

I have wondered for a long time what He will do with me, now at least something has happened.

Send Priscilla and them greetings when you see them or hear from them and thank you so much for the trouble you went to by being so strong while I was at home during the investigation. I know how you feel. I crumble when I think it is my fault and that it is so soon after Brian's death.

Hold tight, please. I also want to tell you now that I'm not in a spot of trouble but a whole lot. 'Friend' Cor van Deventer made sure of that.

I will never get myself out of everything, but I believe now that the Lord has taken me back . . . everything will come right. Please look after my furry children and let them sleep in the room. Give Shalom a hug for me. Thank you for everything.

Stander had left Van Deventer with no real choice. But Stander could not forgive his friend's betrayal. Throughout the court proceedings, Stander cast his former friend long, uncompromisingly hostile glances.

4

The Trial

August 1980

The tables were turned: the man whose career had been based on the conception of prevention and detection of crime now faced his nemesis. After three months on remand in custody, Stander stood in the dock of the Durban Supreme Court. He looked good. Well dressed, he walked tall. But no one but he knew how he felt inside.

Off Beat Cop

André Stander had decided to get to the top. Just like his father, only faster. Much faster.

His had been an off beat decision.

He had reacted aggressively to anything and everything that stood in his way, especially authority. Such was the analysis of Dr J J Bothma, a leading psychologist giving evidence at Stander's sensational trial.

Cor van Deventer, the man who eventually informed on his old friend, said: 'I knew, and he must have known, that I would sooner or later have to report him.' Stander seemed to have a fatal confessional flaw, part of the subconscious death wish perhaps.

Although Stander told his friend that he was responsible for forty hits on banks and building societies, and even asked him to join him, Van Deventer delayed for a few months before telling the Police.

Quizzed during the trial on this delay, Van Deventer explained: 'The fact that he was a very, very good friend and a business partner, he was a captain in the Police Force and in the detective branch, his father was a general in the South African Police at that stage and he comes from a very good home, all made it difficult to believe he was guilty of the crimes he boasted of. I didn't think anyone would believe it if I didn't have proof.'

Although he took the risk of confiding in a friend, in other areas – particularly in the use of disguises – he went to great lengths to cover his tracks.

Plea of Guilty

On his first appearance at the preliminary hearing on the 7th January, he faced an indictment of four charges, in that:

• On the 16th August 1979 he stole a car which he had hired from Budget Car Hire at Louis Botha Airport.

• On the 18th August 1979 he robbed Mrs Patricia Ritchie and Mrs Maria de Marigny of R7 052 at the United Building Society in Durban's Glenwood Centre.

• On the 12th November he robbed Mrs D D Williams and Miss Diane Adams of R14 673 at the Umhlanga Branch of Barclays Bank.

• On the 3rd January 1980 he robbed Miss Diane Williams of R4 944 at the Durban North branch of Barclays Bank.

Later, in the Durban Supreme Court, these charges were boosted to twenty eight including armed robbery, attempted murder, fraud, illegal possession of firearms and an attempt to escape from lawful custody.

During the course of the trail he changed his pleas of not guilty to all counts, to one of guilty to eight counts of armed robbery and one count of attempted robbery at banks and building societies involving R97 500 and to four counts of theft and a forgery and uttering.

In each of the robbery cases, the victims told the court of his disguises.

Mrs Ann Bojanis, a teller at the United Building Society at Randburg, Transvaal, described how a man with dark glasses, a beard, dark hair and wearing a dark blue wind-breaker came into the premises.

'When the man produced a revolver I still didn't realise we were being robbed. I thought the man was only guarding a lot of money which he wanted to bank. It was only when another teller, Mr Garth Cross, asked the man "Can I help you?" and he replied "This is a holdup" that I realised what was happening.'

Cat For The Tom

'The robber,' she continued in her evidence, 'then ordered the tellers to empty all their money into a bag which had the word "cat" written on it.'

The man then ordered the tellers to turn around and he made his getaway.

Another witness at the trial, Mrs Anne Fenton, a teller at the United Building Society, Edenvale, Johannesburg, told how she was relieved of R4 900 during the morning of the 11th August 1978.

'I had just finished counting my money,' Mrs Fenton said, 'when a man at the counter pointed a gun at me and said: "This is a holdup." I gave him all the notes in my till, but he also wanted the money in a drawer behind me. I said he could not have that and he just smiled and walked off.'

She went on to describe him as friendly, neat and well built.

Mrs Fenton activated the bank alarm system which was heard by Mr Geldenhuys in a florist shop nearby. He ran into the building society and was in time to see a man, who struck him as well educated, get into a white Ford Cortina and drive off. He noted the car registration number as TJ 289788.

The bank manager of Barclays Bank in Umhlanga Rocks, north of Durban, said that the man who robbed him of more than R14 000 on the 12th November 1979 was wearing a wig and a false beard. He was sure of this because 'his hair did not look natural and the beard was cut dead straight'.

Mr Duncan Williams, also employed at the same bank, told the court that the robber wore teardrop dark glasses with a metal rim. Indeed, Stander developed something of a fetish for different types of spectacles. Williams said that Stander ordered him to give him five minutes to get away from the bank before raising the alarm.

Williams ignored Stander's brazen request. 'As soon as he was out of the bank I ran to the door and took down the registration number of the Toyota Cressida car as he drove off.'

Stander got away with more than R14 000 from Barclays Umhlanga Rocks.

Mrs Inger Stenesen told how she was robbed of R160 by a masked gunman at the Allied Building Society in Blackheath on the 1st July 1977.

Mrs Stenesen's daughter, who owned a pet shop next door, said she and her mother noted the registration number of the getaway car.

Shown a photograph of Stander taken in Mauritius, Mrs Stenesen said his build was similar to the masked raider.

Mr Deon Smook gave evidence that on the 27th March 1979 he had watched a robbery take place at a Johannesburg branch of Barclays Bank on close circuit television screen. When the lone gunman left, he noted down the registration number of the getaway car.

Mrs Marie de Marigny, a teller at the United Building Society in Durban, gave evidence as to how she and her colleagues were forced to hand over R7 052 to a gunman, who told them not to move for ten minutes so he could get away.

'But while he was still there,' the brave lady said, 'I pressed the alarm which rang in the hairdressing salon next door as well as the police station, and he continued to walk calmly from the building. I ran to the back from where I could see the road and took down the number of the only vehicle in the vicinity which was moving.'

This number matched a false numberplate Colonel Basie Smit found in possession of Stander.

After Stander's arrest Marie de Marigny positively picked Stander out as the robber at an identification parade.

Chance Not Quite

Lady Luck, as well as outrageous pluck, always seemed

to be Stander's mistress. Time and time again chance, not Stander's guile, got him out of trouble.

He had often been careless. In the official diary he was obliged to keep as a detective, he had ringed dates on a calendar and each of those dates coincided with a bank robbery he was charged with committing.

His crime spree, though, almost came to an abrupt end as early as 1977.

A ninety man special police team had been set up to halt the spate of bank and building society robberies plaguing Johannesburg.

On October 1977 Constable Dirk Coetzee was a member of this team, and he was detailed to keep watch on the United Building Society agency in Corlett Drive, Birnam, Johannesburg.

He stationed himself in an office from where he could keep an eye on the cashier and suddenly observed a man, wearing a cap and a jacket with a handkerchief covering the lower part of his face, walk up to the counter and point a gun at the cashier.

'I could vaguely hear him saying to the cashier that he was going to count to three and I realised I had to do something fast,' Constable Coetzee said.

He immediately burst out of the office and opened fire, loosing off three rounds, but ducked back into cover when the robber returned the fire with two shots.

'If I had been a second slower,' Constable Coetzee said, 'he would have hit me in the head and chest.'

When he next ventured from cover his assailant had run for it leaving behind a cloth bank bag and spent cartridges.

Dirk Coetzee to this day cannot be positive in his own mind that the gunman was, in fact, Stander but the cop-turned-crook was later tried and convicted for this attempted robbery to which he pleaded guilty.

Constable Coetzee resigned from the Police shortly after this incident. At the time he said that he never wanted to have to face a repeat of such an experience.

Impervious to Arrest

On the 3rd January 1980, the last day of his one man

crime wave and the day before he was to be arrested by Colonel Basie Smit at Jan Smuts Airport, Stander's obvious conviction that he was impervious to arrest, no matter what he did, brought about a set of circumstances that would probably have made his arrest by police inevitable anyway.

He had contacted Mrs Genevieve van Reenen at Avis car hire, Louis Botha Airport, Durban, on the 2nd January and booked a car for the next day, a flamboyant yellow BMW, under his own name.

When signing the hire agreement the next day he produced his passport as identification and paid for it by Barclay Card.

Another State witness, Mrs Annemarie Brown, told the court how she had joined a queue with her young son, in Barclays Bank, Kensington Drive, Durban.

Her son was cashing a cheque but she wanted to see the cashier who was a friend of hers.

In front of her son was a man. When she greeted her friend she was merely given a strange look in return.

When the cashier finished dealing with the man, who had been robbing her unknown to Mrs Brown, she moved aside to let him pass and then went to the counter.

Afterwards, Mrs Brown said, she followed the man and noted the registraton number of the yellow BMW he drove away in.

A false number plate matching this number was afterwards found in Stander's possession by the Police.

Psychological Make-Up

When Dirk Coetzee resigned after the Birnam raid the Police had lost another man because of the rogue actions of a serving South African Police officer.

Some will no doubt say it was probable that Stander, who was a good shot, had deliberately avoided shooting a fellow policeman, but this is doubtful. Shots from a pistol can never be accurate and the law presumes that shots fired in the general direction of a human being show an intention to kill, which is not an unreasonable presumption.

Was this another facet of Stander's ruthlessness and irresponsibility in his Jekyll and Hyde personality?

During evidence in mitigation of sentence attempts were made to fathom Stander's complex psychological make up. Psychologist Dr Bothma said that Stander underwent a drastic personality change before he started his career of crime. Dr Bothma examined Stander's fights with police bureaucracy, his failed marriage and his relationship with his parents, but he could not explain the personality change.

Maybe he didn't change. Perhaps he was always deep down a rogue elephant. As one Murder and Robbery Squad captain put it: 'I believe he was born bad.'

Dr Bothma said of Stander: 'He had a high intellect . . . I believe Stander knew what he was doing.'

The prosecuting advocate, Gideon Scheitema, agreed. He maintained that Stander should have been given the maximum sentence for his crimes. He told Mr Justice Page, after Stander had been convicted, that it was only with hesitation he didn't ask for the death penalty to be imposed. He asked the court to consider that Stander, as a policeman, had abused his trust and used his knowledge of the weaknesses in the system which he was supposed to defend. And it appeared that most of the robberies had been committed when he was on duty as an officer of the Criminal Investigation Department. His actions, too, had clearly undermined the public's confidence in the Police.

What were Stander's reactions? Shortly after his arrest one of the letters to his distraught parents said.

'I thought I was looking for happiness but I need only have looked up and I would have found it. I looked for trouble and I blame no one. For a long time I have wondered what God would do with me, and now I know.'

Seventy Five Years

Probably the letter was intended for public consumption, not private apology. Whatever the reason, Stander's meeting with God was to be delayed – he escaped the gallows.

Stander was convicted on eight counts of armed robbery, one count of attempted robbery, one count of stealing an identification book, two charges of forgery and uttering, and three alternate charges of theft. He made no statement in his defence, only enough to confirm the admissions which his counsel, Johan Els, had made on his behalf.

Stander listened intently as Mr Justice Page summed up before passing sentence.

He told Stander the sentence he would pass had to suit the crimes of the accused and meet the needs of society.

'The most heavy factor weighing against you,' the judge said, 'is the fact that you were a senior police officer who was trained at the cost of the community to protect the community. You had no dependants and no need for robbing the banks for money which you admitted selfishly wasting on yourself.'

He went on to say that Stander was armed during all the robberies and that he believed he would not have hesitated to use his gun.

'The weapon was loaded in every instance,' continued Mr Justice Page in a precise summation, 'and remarks you made to the witness, Mr Corrie van Deventer, showed your preparedness to use it. The robberies were well planned over a period of two and a half years. False number plates, false names different vehicles and disguises were used.'

He said he did not consider passing the death sentence (armed robbery is a capital crime in South Africa) because nobody was physically injured during the robberies. (It can be a matter of conjecture as to whether or not he would have gone to the gallows had his shots struck Constable Dirk Coetzee during the course of the robbery at the United Building Society in Birnam during October 1977.)

Stander was impassive as sentence was passed. As he put it in another letter, the things that usually made people happy bored him.

The total sentences he was given was seventy five years but with concurrent sentences he would have to serve seventeen and a half years imprisonment – he was going to have plenty of time to get bored.

For robbing Barclays Bank at Umhlanga Rocks on the 12th November 1979 he was awarded eight years imprisonment. Eight years for his hit on a bank in Johannesburg on the 27th March 1979, another eight years on each of five other robbery counts, and two and a half years for theft, forgery and uttering.

Counsel for the Defence, Mr Johan Els, said, that no appeal would be made against sentence at that stage. He commented, according to one press report, that Stander had been prepared for a sentence of about eighteen years.

The date of sentence coincided with General Frans Stander's sixty fourth birthday.

Emotion in Court

In the courtroom his mother, Mrs Violet Stander, sobbed quietly, but wiped away her tears as the judge left the court and her son stepped from the dock.

He kissed and hugged his parents and friends warmly, and they stayed huddled in a small group within the courtroom for more than an hour before he was finally led away to begin his new life as a convict.

Mrs Stander bowed her head in anguished prayer as he disappeared down the stairs leading to the cells.

In the midst of the emotion charged court room, some of the hurt in André Stander's parents was hidden behind their dark sunglasses. But General Stander did not keep all the bitterness and the pain he was feeling to himself.

Like many fathers, he turned his anguish against himself. He blamed his son's actions on himself.

'I forced him to become a policeman against his wishes. He should have left the Police Force long ago,' said the general only minutes after his son had been gaoled.

Stander's boyhood friend, Hennie van der Merwe, who now runs a hardware business in Melville, Johannesburg, at the time bemoaned his old buddy's fate: 'It will kill him, even if he gets half off in remissions. It will kill him unless he can do something like devote his mind to study. Like a wild bird, he cannot be caged.'

Soweto and Sharpeville

After hearing the psychiatric evidence at the trial, General Stander decided to conduct a personal investigation into possible factors which turned his son into a criminal. He spoke to his son's former colleagues and learnt of what he described as the 'horrific' happenings in Tembisa township during the 1976 riots.

'People were shot and André said all he could remember was the blood and the begging for help,' said General Frans Stander. 'It affected him mentally. I went through Soweto and Sharpeville, so I know all about it.'

In mitigation of sentence much was made by his counsel of Stander's alleged experiences during the 1976 unrest.

Stander's mother afterwards brought up the case of former policeman Hendrik Beukes, who was known as the 'Helmeted Robber', as a parallel. He was convicted of robbing Pretoria building societies and banks of R27 000 during 1981. He was sentenced to a total of twenty six years, suspended for five years to run concurrently with a six year term of imprisonment he was already serving for armed robbery.

During his trial Beukes had said he was a member of a special task force that helped to quell the Soweto riots and his turning point had come when 'we fired on rioting youths from helicopters, as if we were hitting buck'.

'Beukes did the same things as André. It makes me so bitter, he did exactly the same things,' said Mrs Stander.

General Stander's attempts to have his son sent for treatment while serving sentence in prison proved fruitless.

He then asked for a retrial: medical experts and family would give fresh evidence on his son's problems and personality defects. This last desperate throw was also in vain.

General Frans Stander said gravely: 'I probably won't live to ever see him in freedom again.' But he was mistaken, for three years later Stander was once more free . . . but this time he had the entire South African Police on his trail.

5

The Big Three

Prison was no place for Stander.

Even while awaiting trial he made plans to escape from custody. He wrote to his former wife, Bekkie.

Hi Bekkie,

This is the loneliest time of the day (night). Everyone asleep except me. My complaints are so serious that they carried in a table and chair for me (don't ask how it fits) and I'm allowed lights ti.'l 10.00 pm to work out my defence.

This morning, out of the blue, I behaved myself almost foolishly and literally cried my eyes out (as you sometimes say). I just felt everything was pushing harder . . . the walls close me in and I can't do anything. Nouja instead of becoming mad, I cried myself silly. I have probably never been so tired as now . . .

Meisie it's Sunday hey, God's day of rest. My day to pack up. I think if I had a weapon this morning, I would have done myself in. I was and am so tired, tired, tired.

Pardon me if I again use your eyes and ears, meisie, I'm just writing from my weak, simple heart and if you want to throw this letter away do so. It's a type of relief to know

*that I can place my cropped up feelings in writing and
share them with you. Maybe you see me now as I really
am, confused, laughable, hey? Oh well, it's also okay.
Everything is so senseless, futile is perhaps the best word.*
Vasbyt, *persevere, just to have to pack up one day.*

I appreciate your friendship, meisie.

I just read the Rapport. *Is it your Vossie de Vos who
had an accident,* meisie? *The face looked familiar, probably him, you know you were almost a rich widow today,
it's not meant sarcastically you hear, I swear I am very
sorry. I hope his wife takes it okay and his kids are okay,
had everything he wanted, pulled away from life. Yes,
God's way is vague.*

*Can you let me know what's going on girl, or is nothing
going on? Will you come visit, are you allowed to? I don't
know. I know what you can actually do, write me a letter I
ask of you and give it enclosed to Hannes. (Hannes is not
identified.) I'll read it sommer there during consultation
(he won't know the contents) then I'll return the envelope
to him and bring the letter back with me in between my defence letters. It is completely safe. Hannes already knows
how to hand over a letter like that to me, and if I know it is
not wise I'll ask him to hold it back. Will you please?*

*Bekkie, ask my father please to make the following ar-
rangements: 1-The car must stay full of petrol. 2-Let him
fill all my extra petrol cans with fuel and put them in the
boot. 3-Ask him please to empty my treasure chest and put
the money under the spare wheel in the Pirana's boot.*

Ag meisie, *I know it's just that car and my own judgement at my father's house that can let me get away. I have
thought everything over a million times and rethought it
and I come to the same conclusion. If you can help me
pack a little case with a sort of short term 'survival kit' that
can be kept in the car's boot together with other things –*
Ag gogga, *I would appreciate it so. Just as much as appreciate you being behind me and that you shake so, Oh, I
love you girl. Please use your obvious expertise concerning the preparation of the Grenada, will you? Let me tell
you why.*

Basie Smit returns on Wednesday from Switzerland. I have already schooled Hannes to corner him as soon as he arrives and to flatter him until he is eight feet long and ten feet wide; he is very conducive to flattery. Hannes will tell him that everyone messed me around while he was away and that I have retained my respect for him. He (Hannes) will get Basie to come and see me, I will ask him to take me for a haircut and to pack a case at home for the trip to Durban.

Basie won't yet be told that we're going to ask for a postponement at the beginning of trial – that's by the way. He'll think we're going to Durban for a long time and I need lots of clothes. At the same time I'll tell him my father would like to meet him. Perhaps even ask him to have supper there. I'll try to sound very enthusiastic about my chances in the case, in a kind of professional camaraderie, you know how.

Bek, I'm sure I'm right when I guess that Basie won't bring the whole army with him. If not, at a certain stage when they don't expect it, I'll simply slip out of the TV room or backdoor. The Grenada must please be ready and stand as your Peugeot did the other day, but out of sight from the lounge window in case someone looks out, there next to the gate (not too skew or the petrol will run out), key in the ignition like the other day.

Ag please meisie, reassure my ma and pa that I won't go against my better judgement and take a chance – then I'd rather wait for your 'mythical rescue operation', you hear. Or is it really like that? I don't know whether you, my pa and ma, aren't just trying to put me off or playing with me. Time is running out.

You can see, it's going to get all the worse, later and the nearer the trial comes the stronger the security gets . . . I'll do as you say and simply keep myself right for anything and not resist, but I know what lies ahead or is available or possible. I can help by setting up an opportunity, do you understand? Don't expect that I be kidnapped like a six year old boy, I don't want your people, whoever they are, to create unnecessary danger that could be avoided if I knew what was coming.

I know these people's minds, Bekkie; remember for fif-teen years I was one of them. I also know their shortcom-ings and I must know what you've arranged.

Even in spite of this, please do the necessary with the car and please check the clutch. You know how my father fin-ishes a clutch within a week. He never takes his left foot off the clutch. Shame, he's a star.

Tell them I won't open myself unnecessarily to bullets in the back.

Bekkie, I swear I feel like the lowest of low scoundrels to have to ask these things of you. I don't even deserve your sympathy (or are you enjoying the adventure). You're also just a weirdo like me, maybe you enjoy the ex-citement secretly, or what?

I always realised I was playing with fire but I've now had enough of gaol – it's not for me, it only awakes shady suicide inclinations which always lay dormant anyway – you know I've philosophised for a long time about life and death and my unimportance in so many things that are im-portant to others. Ag, never mind I won't start philos-ophising again. Life calls from outside and I want to run in the open air again and thank God for the earth and laugh at myself and everything around me. Too much to ask, maybe.

Thank God, however, for you people outside, else I would not have any hope. If it doesn't sound like me, Bek, it's because of the loneliness - being locked up in the small cell – must blame something.

Bekkie, that red bomb (Stander's car) has become the focus point of everything for me. If I get a chance to move in behind its steering wheel, they'll never catch me, that car is like a part of me.

Oh yea, shift the seat back please. My father sits on top of the steering wheel. My hands may be handcuffed – oh yes, please put a long sharp object like a strong nail file or a compass or something like that in the cubbyhole – I can open the handcuffs with that. (You don't perhaps have a pair of false registration number plates somewhere do you, hey?) Joke, joke.

Darling, if you can't come right or get it together, ask my father please to do it. But, you know this, they are alone, unsure and get tremendous strength from your personality. It has always been like that and I would be so pleased if you could be there when Basie Smit and company arrive there with me. It will keep the detectives' eyes busy (You).

Love you, you mad, dilly, lovely, true creature. I am coming back for you as soon as I'm settled.

Please try, darling. Love you forever and a day.

(This is an abridged translated from an Afrikaans letter smuggled from Stander's cell while he was awaiting trial.)

In the hearing of a bail application or alternatively for a transfer to Pretoria Prison, which were both opposed by the State, Stander glibly gave evidence while on oath that he had no intention of escaping from custody and intended to stand trial. He had relinquished his passport to the Police so could not leave the country.

The Police, he said, had hampered him in the preparation of his defence and had placed him in a cell with fourteen convicted prisoners.

No doubt to the horror of the smooth talking Stander, his letter to Bekkie, which had been intercepted by the prison authorities, was handed to him in the dock, while he was under cross examination and he was asked to read it to the court.

Shortly afterwards his counsel, Mr Els, abandoned the application for bail or a transfer.

Once Stander was gaoled, he applied his mind to a study of journalism; perhaps a good career for a bright crook, cynics might say. He had special permission to study in the evenings and at the time of his escape he had two more subjects to write before qualifying.

According to a fellow prisoner Ferdi van den Bergh, 'Everyone wanted to talk to the ex-cop who had turned to the other side of the law. Stander did not want to mix at all with those hooligans and con men.

He preferred to read alone. Although he would answer

questions he would not often be drawn into conversation.'

He made great efforts to improve his standard of English and he often told prisoners that he would leave South Africa and go to another country once he was finished with prison.

'He talked about Cor van Deventer,' said Van den Bergh, 'and this made him hate people but he said he would never kill for it.'

The strange thing is that policemen who are convicted and gaoled for criminal activities are usually badly beaten up by other convicts as soon as an opportunity to do so without detection by warders, arises.

This is for the natural reason that a lot of the criminal inhabitants were put there in the first place by that particular policeman or his colleagues.

In Stander's case, though, it appears there were no criminals there who felt he had wronged them – which says little for his reputation and competence as an officer of the law.

Another ex-convict who knew Stander well and who approached the joint authors immediately prior to the publication of the book said: 'He was a big man with a big rep.' Which in prison jargon means that he was tough and accepted by the rest of the convicts.

Stander hated gaol.

In December 1980 he attempted to escape from prison, apparently with the outside connivance of friends, but the attempt failed and he had three months solitary confinement with spare time to contemplate when he should try his next break.

His father said that representations to ameliorate the conditions of his gaol status had been successful, but his son had escaped before the prison authorities had informed him.

For over three years Stander brooded about how he could escape as he was moved through the prison system. When he was transferred to Zonderwater maximum security prison near Pretoria, he teamed up with Patrick Leigh McCall and Allan George Heyl, who were also serving lengthy prison sentences. The trio were careful not to create suspicion by being seen together too often. Prison authorities carefully ensure that likely conspirators are kept apart.

Escape Artist

McCall was an escape artist. He had once made a dramatic escape from a Cape Town prison by arranging to be thrown out with the kitchen refuse. On his last conviction he had been declared an habitual criminal, and sentenced to the indeterminate sentence. His next escape would have to be the big one. Once free he would need to steal enough so that he could thereafter keep clear of crime and also get out of South Africa.

That, he decided, required a yacht.

He had no sailing experience at all, but for five years before his escape with Stander he had subscribed to yachting magazines. Heyl too had joined in the fervour and he also became an indoor yachting enthusiast.

McCall was an 'A' grade inmate, who was allowed extra access and visitors. He used these privileges to provide Stander with outside contacts. McCall was a resourceful prisoner when it came to fixing things and particularly when it came to escapes.

Stander probably came late to the planning of the yacht scheme, although he must have played an important role in the escape from Zonderwater.

On 11th August 1983 Stander and McCall made their break for freedom while awaiting treatment at the Cullinan physiotherapist. Afterwards both men eluded an extensive police dragnet which included tracker dogs and helicopters.

Police described both men as extremely dangerous. They said Stander was an expert in disguise and it was possible he had changed his appearance.

That must have been the understatement of the year.

Detectives on their trail vowed not to give up the hunt until Stander was apprehended or shot dead.

'We will not give up. We will get him,' a senior detective said.

Although much had been written about what has sometimes been described as the 'evil genius' of Stander, less was known about McCall. He was slender, blond haired, one meter seventy five tall and aged thirty four.

No clear photograph of McCall apparently existed, which was odd because the processing of prisoners' photographs is a routine procedure.

How was it that maximum security prisoners had managed to escape anyway?

Speculation as to the possibility of collusion by prison staff began to be voiced. Stander had a lot of friends. Was this how Stander evaded the police manhunt?

A commission of enquiry was appointed by the Minister of Justice, Mr Kobie Coetsee. It was chaired by Pretoria's Chief Magistrate, Mr H Thompson. Its terms of reference were to investigate:

• The circumstances under which the escape occurred.
• Whether the escape was due to the negligence or dereliction of duty on the part of any member of the Prison Service and,
• Measures (if any) to be taken to prevent a recurrence of such an event.

In mid September, while addressing a passing out parade of prison warders in Pretoria, Minister of Justice Mr H J Coetsee said the report of the commission found there was no collusion in the escape of Stander and McCall. The report had been sent to the Minister earlier that week. So he would not give full details then. The commission found there was one case of negligence and this would be taken further departmentally.

He added that at least two thirds of prisoners held in maximum security institutions were escape risks. The investigation also recommended priority be given to providing medical treatment inside prison walls as often as possible.

Minister Coetsee continued: 'The fact that warders work on a ratio of one to twelve prisoners, compared with certain European countries, such as Denmark and Holland, where the ratio is one to one, does not convince the public either of the difficult circumstances the service has to cope with.'

Many members of the public remained unconvinced.

For the first week after the escape it seemed that Stander stayed on the Reef. Once he rang up an old girl friend living in Boksburg and asked her to pass on a message to his mother.

On the 15th August Stander was identified after he had stopped at a farm near Volksrust and asked the farmer for money for petrol for the motorbike he was using.

Rumour

The wheels of the rumour mill moved into top gear. There was some speculation that he would try to seek out his favourite Alsatian, Shalom.

General Stander held the view that his son would go abroad to take up journalism. With his skills he would probably do well in America.

But Cor van Deventer thought differently – his view was that Stander was after revenge.

'I know him,' he said 'better than anyone . . . he'll be coming after me. I'm sure of it. He sent me word six weeks ago that he was going to get me.'

Although Van Deventer worried about his family, he was not worried for himself. He said he was not a weakling and had once played front row forward for the South African Police first division rugby side.

'I'm armed and ready,' he added.

There was also stories in the Press which suggested Stander might also have the intention of getting back at Colonel Basie Smit who had been responsible for putting him in gaol in the first place.

Colonel Smit, though, dismissed these stories as without substance saying that Stander escaped from prison for his own reasons. He mentioned further that he objected to the press speculation which had been going on, as it upset his relatives.

'I do not,' he said emphatically, 'fear anything.'

And anyone who knows Colonel 'Jumping Jack' Smit would not doubt him in that.

On 24th August 1983 reports came in that Stander had been sighted in Transkei.

Perhaps Stander was long gone in Mauritius, one of his favourite haunts where he was reputed to have stashed some of his money. He had once shown some interest in investing money in a Mauritius hotel chain.

Would Mauritius extradite Stander if he was there?

Narin Rochos, a colonel in the Mauritian Police, said: 'He has done nothing wrong in this country and we don't care what he did in South Africa.'

In fact, he was a long way from Mauritius. He and McCall had rented a house from Mrs Jenny Peters, Number 7, Nina Street, Linmeyer, Johannesburg, on 31st August. It was here that they spent time planning their next criminal exploit. The two spent much of the next two months watching videos.

Escape from Lesotho

In September police received information that Stander had been seen in Lesotho and Captain 'Suiker' Brits was sent there to work with the Lesotho Police.

On the 21st September at about 6.00 pm after a hard day on the lookout for Stander Captain Brits went to a Maseru restaurant for a meal.

While sitting at the table he saw Stander – whom he immediately recognised – enter the room, but he could do nothing about it.

Brits left to get the Police but Stander must have recognised him for by the time he returned with the Lesotho Police his quarry had vanished.

That 'wily old fox,' as one policeman described him, had done it again.

'I could have had him so easily,' said Captain Brits, 'but I couldn't because I was in a neighbouring state. I did not have the Lesotho Police with me.'

This incident again aroused much comment. Sure, he didn't have powers of arrest in Lesotho, but it seems a pity that Brits, who acted quite correctly, didn't grab Stander and leave the diplomatic niceties to be sorted out later. It would certainly have saved the South African Police long months of hard work.

On Saturday the 1st October Stander and McCall rented

another house. This time Number 5, Sixth Avenue, Houghton, one of South Africa's most expensive suburbs.

The landlord, Mr Peter Snyman, was completely taken in by his new tenant's cover story that they were businessmen.

The criminals continued to devour videos. They went to the Southern Suburbs video shop in Turffontein nearly every day between September and December. At first Stander and McCall paid cash for individual videos. Then they took out two fifty rand contracts. They paid up front for the contracts. And they always returned the videos promptly. So there was no need for owner, Mrs Margaret Barkhuizen, to check up on the Linmeyer address supplied by Mark Jennings and Peter Grey.

The very first video that Stander hired on his contract was the *Executioner's Song* – the film version of Norman Mailer's book on how Gary Gilmore insisted on his own execution. That choice of a video seemed to support the police view that Stander himself had a death wish.

Stander was sometimes quite choosy. 'He always wanted recommendations,' said Mrs Barkhuizen. Many of the films on the list are low brow *skiet en donder* videos such as *Dirty Gang, Law and Disorder* and *Violent Breed*. A slightly more upmarket film hired was the futuristic *Escape from New York* - ironic that, in view of Stander's future escape via New York. The gangsters hired about eighty videos in all, paying individually in cash, then they took out two contracts and then went back to individual cash payments.

When Mark Jennings (Stander) first signed for the contract, Mrs Barkhuizen's fourteen year old son, George, asked him whether he was related to the cricketer, Kipper Jennings. Stander used to joke with George as well as Margaret Barkhuizen's other children. 'In a video shop you get hundreds of customers, but he stood out with me and my children,' said Mrs Barkhuizen. 'He was a perfect gentlemen. Clean, well spoken and with a lot of personality. Normally a criminal would throw his weight around. Not him.'

Margaret Barkhuizen obviously enjoyed Stander's custom. 'They were such nice men. I just can't believe that it was them,' she said later. 'The pictures on television don't do them justice at all. They were much better looking.

'I liked Mr Jennings (Stander) so much. We used to joke that he was my boy friend.'

Vice Squad Raid

In one of a number of brazen, or stupid, gestures, Stander and McCall gave their correct address in Linmeyer to the video shop. That was asking for trouble and there was no need to ask for it when trouble could come bouncing in by accident, as it happened one Friday evening when Vice Squad detectives hit the Turffontein video shop in late September. While they were stopping every customer that came in, who should walk in but Stander, South Africa's most wanted man.

According to Mrs Barkhuizen, Stander was completely cool and acted normally. He handed over the video he was carrying, *White Buffalo* starring Charles Bronson, and gave a (presumably fictitious) address to the Police.

The detectives did not recognise him.

Stander's dealings with the shop were discovered when the police found a video receipt in the Houghton shootout address.

On at least five known occasions the Police came face to face with Stander, but except for the Lesotho incident, he was unrecognised.

On 8th October two detectives from the nearby Norwood police station turned up at their Houghton house to investigate a burglary complaint made by previous tenants.

Neither of them recognised Stander who afterwards asked his landlord not to call for the Police again, as they 'bothered him'.

Stander did not want to be bothered because he was busy planning his next dramatic exploit. He was going to spring his old prison mate, Allan Heyl.

The Olifantsfontein Trade Test Centre lies about forty kilometers north east of Johannesburg on the road between Kempton Park and Pretoria.

The centre is a government run complex comprising rows

of long brick buildings with corrugated iron roofs.

It is surrounded by a barbed wire fence about two meters high. However, the effect of the fence is more to define the centre's boundary than to prevent anyone entering or leaving.

It is not a prison but is used to test thousands of journeymen each year to ensure that electricians, plumbers and the like conform to laid down standards.

On a normal day hundreds of cars are parked in the grounds of the centre.

Separate buildings are set aside for the testing of journeymen of each trade. About fifty meters north of the administrative block which is by the entrance is a smaller one than the rest and it was there that Allan Heyl was performing his moulders trade test.

Moulding is dirty work and it seems unlikely that the once aspirant teacher had ideas of choosing this as the basis of a rosy future once out of gaol.

However, the most vital factor for a potential escapee to consider was the relatively little use and remote location of the building. An escape attempt from any of the others, where hundreds of people were performing tests, would have been little short of lunacy.

There was only the tester, Mr A Hornby, another candidate, Mr Izak Smith, and two prison warders, Sergeant Spangenberg and Warder A Potgieter, acting as Heyl's guards.

The escape was worked out meticulously and was executed with military precision.

At 10.30 am on 31st October McCall and Stander parked their Ford Cortina XR-6 a few meters away from the side entrance to the complex, leaving the engine running.

They scarcely attracted a glance as they strode through the grounds and swung open the doors of the building where the moulders were tested.

Another examinee, Izak Smith, said: 'They both had beards and carried guns. They must also have been wearing wigs because they looked identical, like twin brothers.'

Stander merely strolled in, addressed one of the warders

56

by his first name and then ordered him and his colleagues to 'Get on your stomachs.'

Stander grabbed a gun from one of the warders and tossed it over to Heyl who was not wearing handcuffs because of the tests. Instructing the warders to remain on the floor, the trio then ran out and escaped in the Ford Cortina XR-6.

It was cool, precise and audacious. And it worked. The gang of two had become three.

An interesting question is how did Stander and McCall know Heyl was going to be at the centre at the date and time that he was. They must have maintained communication, presumably through visitors to Heyl, after their own escape.

Who was this man whom Stander had risked so much to free?

Heyl came from a similar middle class and stable background as Stander. Also like Stander, he had everything going for him. He matriculated at a school on the Free State gold fields, the Hentie Cilliers Hoërskool, Virginia, and started studying for a teaching degree in Bloemfontein.

Like Stander, Heyl began to reject authority.

A woman close to Heyl said: 'The people in charge there were very conservative and Allan felt closed in by that kind of treatment. Early in his last year of training he did a term of practical teaching. He did so well and the children really liked him,' she said. But then he seemed to have been 'bitten by a money bug' and he dropped out of college.

While working at Woolworths in Cape Town as a trainee manager, he started stealing. Caught, he was sentenced to an eight month prison sentence.

The divorcee he had just married was shattered by his arrest and she divorced him immediately.

Toy Gun

In 1977 Heyl was sentenced to fifteen years imprisonment with hard labour for armed robbery. He had the dubious distinction of pioneering in South Africa, the full face crash helmet as a means of disguise and using high powered motor bikes to escape from the scenes of bank robberies and was eventually arrested by police as he roared away from a robbery on a BMW 1000 cc.

Strangely, Heyl used only a toy gun during those early robberies, but he did snatch real firearms away from guards and tellers.

Why did he risk using a mere toy? Was he, like some say Stander was, apparently reluctant to commit the ultimate of crimes?

Heyl said in court in 1977. 'Physically, it is easy to rob but mentally it is agonising . . . I don't think I would be able to shoot down anybody in cold blood. When I did them (the bank robberies) I was terrified out of my wits.'

But he kept on going.

A commuting criminal, he would travel from his Johannesburg home to Pretoria to carry out his daylight robberies.

Some crimes he committed alone and others with the help of an accomplice, Neville Joseph Cahi, who was eventually sentenced to nine years imprisonment on four counts of robbery and one of theft.

Gun Shop Shooting

The newly reinforced gang needed more weapons. And what better place to get them than in a gun shop? The gang chose the *Kolskoot*/Pot Shot gun shop. This small but well stocked gun shop which incorporated a shooting range, stands on the corner of Aimee Road and Hans Strydom Avenue in Fontainebleau, Randburg.

The gang spent a long time casing it out. For weeks they had their eye on it.

On Friday the 4th November they hung around the shop in the morning. They did the same on the morning of Tuesday the 8th. While they were looking at the merchandise they were also assessing when the busy shop was the quietest. The gang called back on Wednesday and Thursday the 9th and 10th and finally raided it around 3.30 pm on the last day.

This raid was unique as it was apparently the only time that the gang numbered five members. Besides Heyl, McCall and Stander, two other whites acted as accomplices. One was tall and dark and the other was short and fair; both were in their late twenties or early thirties. Neither wore any apparent disguise.

Stander had a few days growth of beard on his chin, besides his big sideburns and moustache.

He was dressed in shorts, a casual shirt, sneakers and sunglasses. McCall had on the same apparel. Stander wore an odd beach hat with a floppy peak. He carried a sports bag. McCall had on an Andy Capp style hat. They did not look too out of place as casually dressed men constantly frequented the gym above the gun shop.

The five men browsed around for a while, looking at the knives and the sunglasses near the entrance of the rectangular shaped shop. While they stood there, a man who later identified himself as a detective walked in. One of the gang turned his back on him. The policeman stood right next to the gang browsing, but after a short time he walked out suspecting nothing. Then the two mystery men supplementing the Stander gang left. They stood outside, apparently counting the customers as they left.

Eventually only one customer remained, Bruce Hay, aged twenty three, who stood looking at gun holsters. Stander, McCall and Heyl went out and came back in again.

Behind the glass topped counter was Mrs Malene Henn, the gun shop owner. Malene is an attractive, forty year old woman who wears her long hair gracefully swept up at the back of her head.

Sometimes her husband, Mike, helps her in the shop and often her fourteen year old son calls in after school, as does her ten year old boy, who sometimes sleeps on the camp bed in the weapons store behind the counter. But that fateful day Malene Henn was on her own.

She always kept a loaded Colt .45 pistol handy. But it was the first time in two and a half years that she had not loaded it. 'I had a premonition that something was going to happen . . . I started crying. I didn't want to come to the shop,' Mrs Henn said later.

But Mrs Henn is no milksop. She was to show more courage than all the men who had looked down the wrong end of Stander's gun. But she would pay for her bravery.

Heyl – the 'passive one' as Mrs Henn called him – stayed in the background. McCall stood next to the counter. He said: 'Lady, have you got any twelve gauge pump action Beretta shot guns?'

Mrs Henn explained that she had. In fact, she said, these one thousand rand guns were on a fifteen percent discount.

McCall smiled. He had a hundred percent discount in mind.

Mrs Henn went into the gun store, a strong room behind the counter, to get a shotgun to show McCall. Suddenly, McCall got on a high stool next to the counter. It toppled over and alerted Mrs Henn. She rushed into the store to grab her Colt.

McCall tried again and scrambled over the counter, leaving a left palm print on the glass which the Police later lifted and positively identified as his.

Malene Henn loaded her pistol and cocked it, then turned around and found herself face to face and gun to gun with McCall, a mere few feet away from her.

Mrs Henn glanced into the shop and saw that her customer, Bruce Hay, had a gun held to his back. Stander was covering him with his short barreled blue magnum, a Ruger .357.

The gangsters were surprised by the bold action of the owner. 'They thought I was just a dumb, stupid woman,' she said later.

'We were eye to eye,' she said. 'I thought, if I shoot you, will they shoot my client?' So Mrs Henn hesitated. That delay was almost fatal.

Later Mrs Henn's husband said: 'She'd had time to get in two shots but she hesitated. She said she still wasn't sure if it was for real. She asked herself if these chaps were playing the fool.'

They were not. McCall shot her. The walls of the strong room muffled the sound.

'I flinched when I saw him pull the trigger.'

The flinching action made her turn sideways and saved her life.

The bullet shot from his silver coloured 9 mm Star model B traversed diagonally upwards through Malene Henn's left arm, struck a rib, penetrated her lung and came out of her back leaving a gaping exit hole.

If she had faced fully towards McCall, doctors say she would have been killed.

She dropped to the floor and lay dazed and shocked watching her own blood stain the cardboard gun boxes crimson. Desperately she tried to staunch the flow of blood from her back.

'Shut up! Shut up! Put the gun down,' Heyl screamed at her.

None of the gang went to her aid, or made a move to help her, and they left her on the floor bleeding and unhelped to die like a dog, as if that was to be her fate.

One day, a few short months afterwards, Stander would himself discover what that was like in his own last few moments of life.

'*Moet ek die ander twee kry* – shall I get the other two?' Heyl shouted in Afrikaans.

Heyl was obviously worried that the shooting had attracted attention. But, in fact, because of the shooting alley there, shots would have been the last thing to cause local alarm.

'*Daar is genoeg vir die winkel* – there are enough for the shop,' replied Stander in Afrikaans.

It was clear to the two hostages that the gang numbered five and not three.

An outsider had witnessed the shooting. A young school girl had walked past the door precisely as McCall fired his shot. She became hysterical and ran to a nearby shop in order to telephone for help.

Meanwhile Stander had tripped Bruce Hay and made him lie on the floor facing the side counter. As he went down his trouser legs rode up slightly revealing an ankle holster. Stander grabbed for the weapon, a 9 mm short Astra Falcon.

The gun had one up the spout. As Stander fumbled – the press stud on the holster flap was difficult to undo at that angle – Hay thought: 'He's going to shoot my foot off.'

Bruce Hay had no chance to use his gun. A police brigadier later told him: 'Be damn glad that you didn't try to use your gun . . . with experts like Stander involved.'

'Lie still. Nothing will happen.' said Stander.

'This one,' Stander indicated to Heyl, 'is behaving himself, carry on.'

The gang then set about looting the shop.

They knew exactly what they wanted and what was in stock. Mrs Henn was forced to point out exactly where the guns and ammunition were kept.

Stander sat on the edge of the camp bed in the store room. Mrs Henn described him as very 'self disciplined'. She said: 'I've never met a person so controlled. He had the whole situation in his hands, but she didn't think he had anticipated the shooting although he took it all in his stride.'

McCall was very nervous and agitated and swung his gun back and forth over the wounded Mrs Henn.

Malene Henn lay on the floor gasping and bleeding, possibly to death, and McCall started yelling at her demanding to know where specific types of ammunition were stored.

'Lady,' he said brutally, 'tell me where it is or I'll shoot you.'

Mrs Henn was finding great difficulty in breathing and could only manage to speak very slowly.

This completely antagonised the impatient and uncaring McCall.

He kept waving his pistol at her and she could see the safety catch was off.

During his gesticulations he suddenly pointed it towards Stander and Stander visibly started as he realised he might be in the line of fire of an accidental discharge.

Showing what Mrs Henn described as 'slight sympathy', he ordered McCall to calm down. 'Leave her, she's going,' Stander said softly but dispassionately.

Mrs Henn believes he was trying to stop McCall from terrifying her more for the reason that the gang still needed her to give information about the shop – not out of compassion for her severely wounded condition.

Press reports later suggested that she felt Stander was trying to stop McCall shooting her again and that his actions thus saved her life. However, Mrs Henn says this was certainly not the case and he didn't care. If he had he would have given her first aid and tried to staunch the blood flow. His words were designed merely to calm down McCall, his partner in armed robbery and attempted murder, so he didn't collect a wild shot himself.

The robbery lasted for just over ten minutes and Mrs Henn remained conscious the whole time.

She remembers looking at Stander and thinking how good looking he was. She later mentioned to her shocked husband when she was in hospital that he had a very good pair of legs.

She mused also as she lay there bleeding and dazed about the different styles of McCall and Stander. McCall was violent and rasping but Stander seemed quite cultured.

While Stander, Heyl and McCall were busy in the shop both Malene Henn and Bruce Hay were convinced the two other gang members were waiting outside the shop.

From his prostrate position Hay could hear the sound of heavy bags being dragged out of the shop. They were loaded with weapons. McCall rushed about the shop trying to clean off his fingerprints. He wiped the two stools but forgot the glass topped counter.

The thieves systematically grabbed a mini arsenal. Their haul included four thousand rounds of ammunition, three twelve bore pump action shotguns, three .357 magnum revolvers, a .223 Mini Ruger, a Colt .45 and two 9 mm pistols.

Stander also indulged his whimsy and grabbed some sunglasses from a showcase.

Stander immediately loaded the pump action shotguns obviously intending that they should use them to blast their way to safety if they met opposition from the Police. Pump action shotguns are used by the South African Police in riot situations and Stander well knew what devastation they can wreak. Carrying one in Tembisa some years before was supposed to have put him off violence.

After gathering up their spoils the gang got ready to leave.

McCall said to Stander: 'What must we do with this one?' He nodded to Bruce Hay.

McCall probably thought that Mrs Henn was dying and Bruce Hay was the only witness.

Would he be shot too? Hay wondered.

Stander said: 'Leave him, let's go.'

As they left, Stander said to Hay: 'Don't move for the next five minutes.' As soon as he heard their footsteps outside, Hay looked up and stood.

No one saw them drive off, although a nearby restaurant manager heard a dramatic screech of tyres.

Once they had gone Mrs Henn managed to get on her feet. She staggered to the door and saw Bruce Hay.

He was understandably in a state of severe shock. Having seen Malene Henn shot he had fully anticipated that McCall was going to murder him. Then, at the last moment, he suddenly found he had been given his life back.

There are two telephones in the shop and she asked him to use one to call the Police and turned to pick up the other one to call her husband Mike, who was busy in the workshop at their house. It was only then that Bruce Hay saw the awful extent of her wounds and the massive bleeding which sogged her clothing and hair.

Unfortunately Mike Henn was using noisy machinery while gunsmithing and he didn't hear the telephone.

While the two victims waited for the emergency services someone walked into the shop but Hay told him to leave. An ambulance (and a journalist) arrived within seven minutes and within ten minutes the place was swarming with policemen.

Mrs Henn was rushed to the intensive care unit of Sandton Clinic. She was lucky and didn't die, although 'the specialist said he couldn't find a reason why she should still be alive.'

She had lost a massive amount of blood, and parts of two of her ribs. The prognosis was that it would take six months before her injuries would be fully healed.

Bruce Hay had thought at the time that Mrs Henn had been killed. He had figured his number might be up too. Did he believe that Stander would have shot him if Mrs Henn had pulled the trigger? No, he said, Stander's responses would presumably have been to turn the gun against Mrs Henn to protect himself and McCall. And after the shooting did he think that Stander would kill him? Bruce Hay thought for a while, 'From him, no . . . . from the other guy, yes.'

'Stander,' said Bruce Hay, 'was to the point . . . in total control.' He described the operation as 'obviously well planned'. Stander had led it with military precision. Hay had noted the white Cortina XR-6 with black louvres on the back outside the shop (he owns a white Cortina himself, and made a special mental note about the high performance XR-6). The car was full of people, he observed. He also confirmed that more than three raiders had hit the shop. He heard Stander say that 'Four is enough for the shop' at one stage in the raid.

While lying on the floor Hay assumed that the fourth man was at the door and a fifth in the car.

'There were definitely more than three people in that shop,' he said.

But why didn't he tell the Police about it? He thought carefully. 'Do you know, they didn't ask me.' (Mrs Henn, however, says she told Police that more than three gangsters were involved.)

Mr Hay says that the gang, having put themselves in the criminal situation that they were in, couldn't avoid shooting Mrs Henn when she resisted. It was either them or her and unfortunately she hesitated on the trigger.

Mrs Henn, who lives with guns and who has been on a combat shooting course, says she hesitated because she was worried that her customer, Bruce Hay, would have been shot by the gang. This hesitation all but cost her her life.

Would she hesitate if faced with the situation again?

'This time I would pull the trigger. I would kill him outright. I wouldn't waste a second to think of the hostage with a gun in his back. I'll think of myself first.'

Just after the raid some doubt was expressed as to who really shot Mrs Henn.

Initial press reports suggested it was Stander. There was romantic speculation that Stander was very angry he had been blamed for the incident and that this could start a rift between himself and McCall.

There was even a story that Stander had indignantly telephoned the Police to tell them he was innocent.

But, to clear the haze of Robin Hood romanticism felt by some people, the Police are quite categoric that he didn't.

Mrs Marisa Reinertz, Secretary to Editor of *Beeld* said that Stander telephoned and said: 'I did not shoot her. Do you understand?'

After a few seconds he repeated himself, but when asked more questions he rang off.

Brigadier Jan Fourie, Divisional Criminal Investigation Chief on the East Rand, said he strongly doubted that it was Stander who telephoned.

Most likely explanation is that it was a crank, out to whitewash the tarnished image of Stander for he certainly showed no remorse when the shooting happened.

Photographic identification by Mrs Henn, comparison of a palm print lifted from the glass counter and ballistic evidence conclusively confirmed that it was McCall who fired the shots. The palm print was a big mistake on his part. It was only after McCall had climbed over the counter that both Stander and McCall donned gloves which they had in the sports bag.

Mrs Henn still serves behind the counter of the gun shop. But now she keeps enough weapons loaded and readily available to repel an army.

She still has nightmares about Stander coming back to the shop, but is remarkably calm and lucid when recalling the traumatic events.

Malene is an ex-teacher who has studied psychology. She is very sure of her own feelings and has not withdrawn into a shell as a result of her dreadful experience.

Except for the well armed police professionals who were ready and waiting in Houghton and Fort Lauderdale to tackle Stander, she was one of only two people who had the sheer gutsy courage to face up to him.

She is a brave and determined woman. Today she angrily reflects on the possible effects on her two children – not the dangers to herself – when she challenged the Stander gang. Besides the physical wound she said she is still injured psychologically.

In one of the many coincidences in the Stander story, Mrs Henn's gun shop is next door to the White Pigeon Roadhouse, owned by Mr George Nicholoau. Mr Nicholoau bears a striking resemblance to André Stander, although he is shorter than the gangster. The roadhouse owner was stopped by detectives at Jan Smuts Airport on the lookout for Stander. This might be one explanation for a reported sighting of Stander at the airport. Certainly, Stander mania produced a number of countrywide false sightings.

A teenage schoolgirl, who was interviewed by the Police immediately after the gun shop raid, said that she had seen the white Cortina Interceptor with camping gear in the back at midday in the area. A number of unfortunate and certainly innocent campers were later grabbed by the police near Pretoria as a result.

New Arsenal

With their new arsenal the Stander gang would be able to hold out against a small army, but what on earth did they intend to do with such an impressive array of weaponry?

The Police were clearly worried. A special task force was set up to smash the Stander gang. Helicopters were brought in to look for the white Ford Cortina XR-6 in which they had escaped. But false alarms poured in. Stander, said the Police, was moving fast. 'He knows the Witwatersrand area well. He will not be like a sitting duck waiting to be shot.'

Police were wasting their time looking at campers, though, for the Stander gang was not hiding in the hills. They were sitting smugly undisturbed in the luxury of plush Houghton.

They were not planning to commit an individual super crime either, a South African version of the Great Train Robbery. No, they intended escalating their campaign of robbery.

They would soon be dubbed the 'bank hoppers'.

6

Bank Hopping

August 1983 – January 1984

Bank hopping was nothing new to André Stander. He had done it successfully before. His previous hops had earned him almost a hundred thousand rand.

During the many idle hours he spent in prison musing over his downfall and dreaming of his escape, Stander must have refined his bank hopping concept. He clearly came to the conclusion that more money could be made in less time if he hit larger banks and building societies – but to do this successfully he needed partners.

This might seem to be merely a logical progression from his old method of operation, but for Stander it would have been an important decision. Betrayal by his best friend Cor van Deventer had put him in gaol and he was loathe to trust anybody but himself, for he was characteristically a loner.

But the decision had been made and the stage was set. The gang had been formed, hideouts had been established and an arsenal of weapons grabbed.

Stander, the undoubted leader, was ready to start work.

It is often said that the simplest plans work best. The bank hopping concept – despite its inherent dangers – was no exception.

Their robbery spree had begun early on the 19th August 1983, while the gang was still had a core of only two men, with a lightning attack on the United Building Society in Hendrik Verwoerd Drive, Randburg.

They held up the young teller, Mr Mark Campbell, at gunpoint and then ran for it after grabbing R20 000 in cash.

This was the first of five robberies Stander and McCall committed together before, according to the Brixton Murder and Robbery Squad Chief, Brigadier Manie van der Linde, McCall was forced to drop out of the team after sustaining a broken leg and jaw during a motor car accident.

The robbery at Randburg marked the beginning of a crime spree which would leave the South African Police stunned, frustrated, but determined to catch the gang.

Mrs Remona van Staden of Thistle Street, Benoni, advertised her 1979 silver grey Ford Cortina in the 'for sale' columns of a newspaper.

During the afternoon of the 1st September a man, who she afterwards identified as Stander, called at her house and expressed interest in buying the car.

He identified himself as a policeman from Durban and gave his name as Mostert. He said he was attending a course in Johannesburg. Stander still had Constable Mossie Mostert's police identity card.

After looking the car over he asked to take it for a test drive. Mrs van Staden agreed, and got into the front passenger seat while Stander took the wheel . . . her young daughter Francina, aged twelve, got in the back.

After going around the block Stander steered back into Mrs van Staden's drive.

Remona van Staden got out, as did Francina, but Stander stayed in the seat, slammed the gears into reverse and backed hurriedly down the drive.

A Real Bloody Heroine

But quick thinking and attractive Remona was just as fast in her reactions as the feline fit Stander and she threw herself back into the front seat.

Stander braked the car and produced a pistol which he menaced her with.

'Nou gaan ek jou doodskiet - Now I'm going to shoot you dead,' he said.

In a smooth action which was to later prompt a policeman to describe her as 'a real bloody heroine', she knocked the gun from his hand, grabbed it in the fumble for repossession and tossed it out of the window.

Both Stander and she jumped from the car and there was a mad scramble for the weapon lying on the ground.

Unfortunately, Stander was able to shove Remona van Staden out of the way and regain possession of the gun.

It was clear that he had the upper hand and further resistance would have been foolish, so there was nothing the plucky lady could do but stand there and watch Stander drive away in her car.

On Friday 16th September the bank hopping by Stander and McCall began and they robbed three banks within a single hour.

Their first target, at 9.05 am, was the United Building Society, Central Avenue, Kempton Park, where they robbed Mrs Ansie Jones and Miss Lynn McGuire of R8 000 which was scooped from their tills.

From there they hopped to Barclays Bank, De Korte Street, Braamfontein, where twenty five minutes later at 9.30 am they held up the teller Mr C Tenson and stole R10 610 from him.

Their final job of the hour was Barclays Bank, President Place, Jan Smuts Avenue, Rosebank, where a mere forty five minutes after they had started their day's work at 9.30 am, they strolled boldly into the banking hall and held up the teller, Mrs Duisie du Mughh and lifted R12 700 from her.

An Unlucky Break

At 4.30 am on Monday the 10th October stockily built Neville Peterson was driving a breakdown truck of the Hilton Silver Towing Service along the Main Reef Road in Amalgam near the M-2 west onramp when he spotted a silver grey three litre Ford Cortina, registration number GSN 241 T, in front of him, which had clearly just crashed into a pillar.

The right front and side of the car were badly damaged. Steam was still escaping from the damaged radiator.

Neville Peterson drew up, jumped out and went to the aid of the white driver, a man wearing a mohair jacket and an Andy Capp style hat.

'You all right?' Do you need any help?' he asked the man who was clearly in pain.

'I've just broken my leg,' the injured driver said, 'but I'll be okay.'

'How you going to be okay if you've broken your leg?' asked Neville Peterson not knowing if the man was joking or not.

The man was insistent and even refused the offer of a lift and a tow.

Well, bugger you then, Neville Peterson thought and got back into his rig and drove off.

Hilton Silver Towing Service has the contract with the Johannesburg Traffic Department so he knew it was likely he would be called back to tow the vehicle in later on anyway.

As for the man with the broken leg, well, he could sort himself out if he felt that way.

Later at about 9.00 am, as he had predicted, he received a call from the Traffic Department to tow the damaged Ford in.

The injured driver had been taken to the Johannesburg Hospital.

The next day, Tuesday the 11th October, three men, in a very distinctive BMW 320i, arrived at the Hilton Silver Towing Service yard in Basalt Road, Amalgam, which is around the corner from the accident scene.

Neville Peterson and Louis Hamman spoke to the men. They didn't know them and the driver of the accident car was certainly not with them.

One of the men who seemed to be the spokesman introduced himself as Derek Johnson of 129 Fourth Street, Lynwood, Pretoria and said he was the owner of the wrecked Ford.

'Could I collect a few things from the car as the driver is

in hospital?' he asked.

'But certainly,' was the answer, and both Messrs Peterson and Hamman watched without particular interest as the trio removed goods and loose items from the car's interior and a suitcase from the boot.

'Thanks,' said Mr Johnson.

'But what do we do with the car?' asked Louis Hamman.

Mr Johnson shrugged and told him the insurance would sort matters out, but to meanwhile take it to Currie Motors Panel Beaters in Salisbury Street, Johannesburg, whom he dealt with. This was done.

The three men left. Unknown to both Louis Hamman and Neville Peterson, Mr Johnson was Stander.

D Johnson was a favoured *non de plume* of Stander. He was using it when he was a passenger on a flight from Durban, at the conclusion of which he was arrested by Colonel Basie Smit for armed robbery in January 1980. Labels in that name were plastered all over his luggage, too.

Needless to say, the car wasn't his either. It had false number plates and was the one he had stolen from Remona van Staden and had very nearly come unstuck himself because of her resistance.

The facts would remain unknown to the men at Hilton Silver until they were told by one of the authors during the writing of this book.

At Currie Motors, Mr Wesley Lloyd, the paintshop general manager, booked in the car with Mr Derek Johnson marked as the owner, and left it in the yard pending instructions which never came.

Stander, with his knowledge of police procedures and the ponderous way that insurance companies go about their convoluted business, must have been well aware that it was likely the car would remain at Currie Motors panel beaters without a question being raised until his mystery accomplice left hospital, and he was right.

The car was not discovered to belong to Mrs Remona van Staden until after Stander was killed and McCall long buried. It was only when Currie Motors panel beaters reported to the Police the existence of the long abandoned car.

Fortunately for Mrs van Staden, although the car was a write off, the insurance company paid her out in full.

The Johannesburg Traffic Department have no record of the accident and no record of the driver, who he was and whether or not he was ambulanced to hospital.

This should cause no surprise as only one vehicle was involved in the accident and little police notice is taken of such events, unless there is a clear case of negligent driving or drunkenness.

It seems that Remona van Staden's car and certainly the name D Johnson were completely unlucky for Stander.

It was around this time that Patrick McCall had his accident. His leg was broken and his jaw smashed. According to police information, he was admitted to the Johannesburg Hospital where he remained as a patient for some weeks. However, this cannot be confirmed as details of records relating to patients at government hospitals are confidential. It seems unlikely he was the driver of Remona van Staden's car when it was written off, as he certainly was not suffering from a broken limb or limbs when he helped to spring Heyl on the 31st October, and when he left a palm print at Mrs Henn's gun shop on the 10th November.

The hospital won't confirm his hospitalisation. The Police, however, have confirmed they have a photograph of McCall with his leg in plaster and his jaw wired up, which was passed to them by an informer.

His treatment at Johannesburg Hospital was obtained under an alias as was the wiring up of his broken jaw by a Johannesburg dentist.

Mrs Margaret Barkhuizen of the Southern Suburbs Video says that the last time she saw Patrick Leigh McCall he came into the shop with both legs in plaster.

'He told me he had been in a car accident and had just spent two weeks in intensive care.'

Stander continued with Heyl alone, even though the latter was reputed to be the weak link in the outfit. But the two soon proved to be a highly successful team.

Back to Business

On the 28th October at 11.00 am Stander and McCall

strolled into the Trust Bank at Benoni, held up Mrs B M Style and escaped with R9 845.

The gang had more than R40 000 in the kitty by the time Heyl joined them. After securing his escape from the Olifantsfontein Trade Test Centre, the gang remained in the area for four days.

On the 4th November a lady was driving in the area of Olifantsfontein when she was forced off the road by an XR-6 Ford Cortina Interceptor containing three white men.

One, whom she later identified as McCall, jumped out, got into her car and held a pistol to her head.

McCall told her to get out as he wanted the car, but he then noticed the gauge showed the tank was empty. He looked around and grabbed a bag containing R3 850 instead.

He then got back into the car with his accomplices and drove off.

To guarantee the success of the bank hopping raids, the gang needed more weapons and the gun shop raid on Thursday the 10th November provided their needs.

On Tuesday the 29th November Stander and Heyl brazenly hit three financial institutions – hopping from the East Rand to the central Johannesburg area to complete their haul.

Their first target was the United Building Society in Voortrekker Street, Alberton, in the middle of the central business district.

Stander and Heyl strolled into the premises at about 9.15 am. Heyl took up position at the door to keep guard while Stander, gun in hand, ordered the four tellers behind the counter to put all the money into a blue plastic bag.

The getaway car, a blue Ford Cortina XR-6, was waiting for the two bank robbers outside. They had left the engine running.

The stickup had gone off faultlessly and the two men made their getaway more than R2 000 richer.

From Alberton they drove to the quiet suburb of Blackheath to the north west of Johannesburg after changing their getaway vehicle en route.

At 9.45 am Stander and Heyl walked into the Barclays Bank in D F Malan Drive.

They looked to all appearances like businessmen in their sports jackets and casual clothes.

In a repeat performance of the earlier robbery, Stander threatened the tellers at gunpoint, then moved along the counter ordering each teller to drop their money into his bag. While this was going on Heyl stood at the door monitoring the bank staff.

By this time East Rand Murder and Robbery Squad detectives had arrived at the scene of the first robbery completely unaware that another crime by the same gang was in progress elsewhere.

This second robbery brought the two robbers another financial harvest, this time R17 560.

As soon as Stander and Heyl had left, the bank alerted the Police and soon detectives from the Brixton Murder and Robbery Squad detectives were racing to the scene.

As in the case of the East Rand Murder and Robbery squad, they did not suspect that the men they were after were about to pull a third one.

Near the main entrance of the popular Rosebank Shopping Mall are branches of the Trust Bank, the Standard Bank and the Allied Building Society. The gang could have chosen any one of them, but the Trust Bank – possibly the least busy of the three – was elected for the dubious honour.

Mr Danie Visagie, a temporary teller, had just locked up his till and left the bank briefly to buy a magazine.

On his way out he unsuspectingly brushed past the Stander gang who were on their way in.

When he returned it was to find the bank robbed and the bank marauders gone only by a matter of seconds.

The teller who had been robbed of R1 500 was still standing in a state of shock.

Danie Visagie's locked till, which contained approximately R10 000, was still intact.

In one of those ironic twists of the Stander saga, Danie Visagie is the brother of Mrs Malene Henn who was shot by the gang at her Randburg gun shop on Thursday the 10th November.

Brazen Disregard for Safety

This last attack of the day showed the gang's brazen disregard for their own safety. The Rosebank Mall is well protected by security guards and one of them, an African man armed with a truncheon and carrying handcuffs, was standing only a few meters away from the bank when they struck.

He saw them leave but, as he didn't know a robbery had just occurred, he took little notice. In any case even if he had, he would have been able to do little against the Stander gang with his truncheon.

The two crooks walked out of the building into Craddock Avenue, normally a no parking area, where their car was waiting. They had not been ticketed – the robbery had taken such a short time.

Less than a week later, on Sunday the night of 4th December, Stander and Heyl pulled their most daring holdup.

The various concourses at Jan Smuts Airport are extremely busy on a Sunday night with dozens of local and international flights arriving and departing. The Volkskas Bank agency, like all airport banks, has many thousands of rands passing over their cashiers' counters, as travellers convert their currency and travellers cheques.

The two tellers on duty, Brian Kenny and Peter Hillary Harris, were suddenly confronted by Stander and Heyl at 7.15 pm. Like all the gang's victims they handed over all the cash they had without argument. This time, though, it was not only money they were after, and before leaving Stander took the Books of Life belonging to the two tellers as well as their passports.

The passports were to be used by the gang later.

The miscreants strolled out on to the concourse, mingling with the crowd before disappearing with R71 305 in cash. They also nobbled about R20 000 worth of foreign currency.

What struck the tellers most was the icy calm manner in which the robbery was executed.

Two customers waiting in the bank were actually unaware that a holdup was in progress until the alarm was raised after the two armed plunderers had disappeared.

Railway Police officers were quickly at the scene but Stander and Heyl had got completely clear.

Descriptions of the robbers given by the tellers and their method of operation gave the Police one of their first good indications that their former comrade was the man they were after.

From that time on the gang struck almost daily. Stander and Heyl were to pull twelve jobs between them within a month – between Tuesday the 29th November and Tuesday the 27th December.

The Yellow Porsche

International Cars in Louis Botha Avenue, Johannesburg live up to their name and the hint of plush snobbery in the type of luxury cars they sell, but when they put the canary yellow Porsche Targa on display for R32 000, even they decided they had come up with something pretty special.

This it seems was the feeling of Mr Geoffrey Marshall, a suave and rich young executive, who spoke to Mr Luciano Sartori, one of the showroom owners, about it on Wednesday the 14th December.

Mr Sartori explained all the luxury features of this exotic car to the keenly interested Mr Marshall. There were only four in South Africa and it was the only one in canary yellow. It was incredibly high powered and capable of reaching speeds in excess of one hundred and eighty kilometers an hour. Quite an acquisition indeed and only R32 000.

The price didn't frighten Mr Marshall and Mr Sartori took him out for a test drive.

They left the showroom with Mr Luciano Sartori behind the wheel of the smooth as satin motor car.

'Could I test drive it?' Mr Geoffrey Marshall asked when they reached the Corlett Drive onramp to the M-1 Motorway.

'Of course,' Mr Luciano agreed, because, after all, one did not sell an expensive car every day.

He got out and the smooth Mr Marshall slid over into the

driving seat, his foot touched the pedal and the owner was left only with a rear view and then only a memory of the fast accelerating yellow motor car as it quickly disappeared from sight.

Even after that Mr Sartori still couldn't believe that the sophisticated Mr Marshall had actually stolen his car and he walked back to the showroom and made some other checks before finally calling the Police.

Perhaps if he had realised sooner that Mr Marshall was really Mr Stander, he would have contacted them earlier.

When Mr Sartori finally got it back from the Police two months later, it was to find it in immaculate condition with only four thousand, five hundred extra kilometers on the clock. The oil and water were topped up and the car well polished. Because of the notoriety Stander had gained, too, Mr Sartori was able to bump up the price.

The gang's brassy boldness created a major headache for the investigating officers who began working around the clock to apprehend the robbers.

A special control room was set up at Brakpan with six very experienced officers from other divisions under Captain (soon to be promoted to Major) Gerrit Viljoen but this was later moved to the more centralised position of the Brixton Murder and Robbery Squad headquarters, under the command of Brigadier Manie van der Linde, who would coordinate the whole operation.

Give Them Enough Rope

For a long time the Police were reluctant to admit that the audacious bank hoppers were the Stander gang. With each daring raid, the police tried harder to catch them, but as time passed they grew more exasperated.

In the early stages of the police campaign, General Zietsman said: 'They have evaded us so far. But give them enough rope and they will hang themselves.'

Perhaps give them enough money would have been more apt.

Despite a nation wide hunt, the toll of plundered banks mounted.

The rewards mounted too. The Clearing Bankers' Association of South Africa offered R5 000 reward for each criminal caught.

The innocent always suffer most and the agony of Stander's family escalated as well. Mrs Violet Stander said: 'This whole thing is killing us. Every time we turn on the radio or watch television we are bombarded with allegations levelled against our son. It is a lot of nonsense.'

But the Press knew a good story when it saw one. Gradually, the saga of the bank hoppers grew into a major story.

Tense Moments for Nothing

The sightings increased too. One minute Stander was in Cape Town, the next he had been seen playboying in Mauritius. Suddenly, as well as being a bank hopper, he was portrayed as a resort hopper.

This is the 15th one today – 'Cut it shortish at the side with a wave, and sweeping across the forehead, die it red and give the moustache an orange tint'.

Some innocent unfortunates suffered as well. A Randburg man who drives a car similar to the gang's was chased by police 'waving guns' and forced off the road near North Riding.

79

On another occasion, as the result of a tip off, police in a smooth operation cordoned off two city centre blocks in Pretoria.

Several people felt sure they had seen Stander.

Shots were heard, but after an hour's search the cordon was abandoned when it was discovered the weapon causing all the trouble was a high velocity gun used to drive nails into walls on a nearby LTA Construction site, according to the foreman, Mr Leonardo de Gennero.

As the manhunt expanded and helicopter searches became commonplace, his father maintained that his son was abroad. General Stander said: 'He knows I was a professional policeman and he is not sure if my loyalties still lie with the Force. But André need not fear . . . after what they have done to him. I would never inform on him!'

Despite a certain amount of sympathy for the old man's agony, the public attitude – especially that of the victims of Stander's raids – was hostile to the pronouncements on his son.

Mr Mike Henn, whose wife, Malene, was shot by the gang in the raid on his gun shop in Randburg, was understandably incensed by statements which, according to the Sunday papers, both General Frans Stander and Mrs Violet Stander made.

They alleged that General Stander 'vowed that even if he knew he wouldn't reveal his son's whereabouts' and Mrs Violet Stander said if her son was still in the country and if he was responsible for the crimes he is believed to have committed, he must leave the country as soon as possible.

Mr Henn said the comments made by General Stander were unheard of. 'He, an ex-policeman who reached the highest rung, is putting the life of his son over that of other people, while Malene put her life at stake to prevent the gang from getting to the weapons.

'General stander was embarrassing the South African Police with such behaviour. If he was not a policeman,' Mr Henn continued, 'one could maybe understand it. But while he was a policeman he must set an example to hundreds who had to follow.

'How can he (General Stander) put the life of his son, who is a criminal, over that of innocent people and policemen?'

A spokesman for the Police Public Relations Office did not want to comment on statements made by Stander's parents to the Sunday Press.

He said only: 'It is a crime to help another to commit a crime' – an apparent reference to a comment by Stander's father that 'he would not say where his son was even if he knew'.

Later a senior police officer commented that the provocative statements made in newspapers by General Stander were sending Stander to his death.

Reacting to reports which quoted General Stander as advising his son to flee and not give himself up, the chief of the East Rand Criminal Investigation Department, Brigadier Jan Fourie, said:

'If it were my son I would tell him to give himself up. There's still a chance that he (Stander) can be rehabilitated.'

Free Wheeling Contacts

It was rumoured that the gang regularly contacted friends and family by telephone and sometimes even made visits. McCall was said to often complain to members of his family about being lonely – a constant diet of videos and girls from escort agencies must soon have palled.

On one occasion McCall rang up an old school friend, whom he had not seen since 1978. McCall asked him whether he had any printer's ink for a passport, but the friend said that he could not help McCall in any way, otherwise his own family would be in jeopardy.

These free wheeling contacts, usually by telephone, and McCall's alleged stay in hospital suggested, by their arrogance, that they didn't think the South African Police would ever catch them.

General Stander meanwhile still insisted that his son had left the country: 'André is long gone.'

But he was far from gone and was still based in Johannesburg's comfortable northern suburbs, masterminding the most persistent blitz on banks and building societies that South Africa had known.

Five days after the airport hit on Friday the 9th December the gang struck again, this time four strikes on one day.

Their first target was the Natal Building Society in Odendaal Street, Germiston.

Miss Tracey Kimper and another teller, Mrs Saaiman Heath, were tackled by two armed men who ordered them to put all their money into a bag.

After the robbery the gunmen were seen to make good their escape in a light blue Cortina, registration number FMT 417 T.

On this robbery they made R3 562.

At 11.30 am the gang walked into Standard Bank in De Korte Street, Braamfontein.

They robbed the teller, Mr T Pensen, of six thousand, nine hundred and twenty rand.

Again Stander approached the counter while Heyl kept watch at the door.

They fled before the alarm could be sounded.

As bank security personnel and Murder and Robbery Squad detectives converged on the scene, the two rogues – Stander and Heyl – had arrived at Barclays Bank in Jorrissen Street only two blocks away. Using the same *modus operandi* they held up Mr Brian O'Donnell and several other tellers and customers, grabbed R9 900 in cash and escaped in a waiting getaway car.

Less than two hours after the second robbery, and while the Police still swarmed around the second bank taking statements from employees and clients, the fugitives from prison pitched up back in Rosebank – the scene of their Trust Bank robbery on the 29th November.

Minutes later they ducked out of the United Building Society in Craddock Avenue after snatching R15 190 from the teller Miss C Okell. They stuffed it in the now familiar blue bag.

Too Easy

It had become all too easy. They had not yet been faced with any heroics by bank or building society staff and all of them had handed over the money meekly and with the minimum of fuss.

The only people who had fought back were two of the gentler sex, the courageous Malene Henn and Remona van Staden.

Hundreds of people should have spotted them during the holdups, but no one, up until that time, had positively identified them.

Their use of various types and shades of wigs and glasses as disguises made it very difficult, if not impossible, for a clear identification to be made of the gangsters.

Continually raiding banks in close proximity to each other would have been too much of a giveaway, so they kept the Police guessing by hopping from Reef town to town and suburb to suburb, tackling establishments of different sizes and quality.

In spite of their persistent use of the blue Ford Cortina XR-6 as a getaway car this, too, had not brought them any nearer to arrest.

The car should have been a dead giveaway. Only two hundred of these fifteen thousand rand cars had been built in South Africa. Three carburettors, although they gave rapid acceleration, also provided a very distinctive engine growl.

On Monday the 19th December, ten days after the last raid, Stander and Heyl pulled a single job, the last before the Christmas holidays.

At 12.25 pm two of the gang, both wearing sunglasses, walked into the United Building Society in Boksburg and held up Mrs Sandra Davies and two of her colleagues with guns.

They appeared to be completely undeterred by the fact that there were several other customers in the building society at the time.

They demanded that all the cash be handed over to them and, after the tellers' drawers had been emptied, they walked out.

They were seen making their getaway in a blue Ford Cortina which this time showed the false registration number of

FMT 471 T.

On this robbery they made good their escape with a total of R19 800.

Sleeping Partner

All this time McCall's leg was still in plaster and his jaw wired up, forcing him to remain a sleeping partner in the gang's activities.

Stander and Heyl had laid their lives on the line nine times and were to pull three more spectacular heists before McCall returned to the team.

Having taken a week off for Christmas, the gang turned its attention to Pretoria.

On Tuesday the 27th December Stander and Heyl followed their now established routine. They got into their powder blue Ford Cortina XR-6 and drove to the capital city.

They arrived at the Sunnyside branch of the Trust Bank in Esselen Street at 10.30 am, parked their car and went inside.

Sunnyside is primarily a residential suburb, close to the centre of Pretoria. It has scores of blocks of flats, cinemas and a shopping complex and several streets of shops, similar to although not quite on the same scale as Hillbrow.

Stander and Heyl adopted their customary roles inside the bank and held up Mrs Ansie Kent and Miss Karen Beinecke. A few minutes later they strolled out with more than R16 000.

They then headed south for Johannesburg, stopping off at the Barclays Bank in Verwoerdburg fifteen minutes later.

Five minutes later they doubled back towards Kempton Park, which was the area Stander knew best. His former police station was only a few blocks away from the Allied Building Society in Kempton Park's West Street – their next target.

Delivering their orders to Mrs Tertia Fourie – with a mixture of calm and menace which didn't allow any misunderstanding – Stander and McCall relieved her of R13 900.

Their spoils for Tuesday the 27th December amounted

to almost R60 000. Not at all bad for a few hours work.

McCall's leg was by now healed. During a two week break, the gang travelled to Cape Town to buy a yacht. In the same period they hired another house in Houghton and Stander began entertaining Sue Hewitt.

Then on Thursday the 19th January McCall was back in circulation. Now they were three and the game became easier; one to guard the door and keep an eye on the getaway car, one to watch the customers and staff and the third to threaten the tellers and loot the tills.

At 11.15 am they struck the Standard Bank at De Korte Street, Braamfontein. This high density city area was very familiar territory as they had raided it before.

The tellers, Mrs Cornelia van Tonder and Mrs Sarah Richards, were forced at gunpoint to oblige the gang with the contents of their cash drawers. This was one of their biggest hauls yet, a total of R30 574. But it was only the start. The three armed bandits were to make their biggest day's haul in the five months they had been operating.

Fifteen minutes after leaving the Standard Bank, De Korte Street, the blue Cortina pulled up outside the Barclays Bank in Louis Botha Avenue, Orange Grove, about ten kilometers away. One of the most congested roads in Johannesburg, Louis Botha Avenue carries rush hour traffic to the city centre. Although this was out of the peak period, the road was still busy. Yet they found a parking space near their target.

Barclays in Orange Grove is one of the larger suburban branches of the Bank, serving a number of nearby residential suburbs.

Undeterred by the fairly large number of staff and clients in the bank, the trio performed their normal routine. They held more than a dozen staff members and customers under their guns while the job was done.

But when a customer, Doron Peleg, made a move, Stander turned towards him.

'Don't try it,' he warned.

The gang was so quiet and businesslike that few members of the staff or the public realised what was happening.

The bandits went from teller to teller ordering each to put the money from their cash drawers into the bag.

A woman who was in the bank at the time said: 'I don't understand how they could have been so casual about the whole thing. I was petrified.'

Another lady customer remarked: 'I had this horrible feeling in my stomach. It was terrible.'

Their haul was R48 202 but still this was not enough.

They could have headed towards their hideouts but they did not. They had another objective before quitting for the day – Nedbank in Fifth Street, Wynberg – an industrial suburb just north of Johannesburg. It took them about ten minutes to get there. Dozens of small to medium sized factories are situated in Wynberg and the banks there deal in larger sums of cash than the average.

Biggest Haul

The gang were now set to make their biggest cash haul of the entire money making operation. A total of R88 404 was to await them.

For the Stander gang the fact that Nedbank at Wynberg could only be reached by going up a flight of stairs presented no problem. They parked the getaway car outside and walked into the building.

By this time, Brixton Murder and Robbery Squad detectives, already hard pressed investigating the first two robberies, had arrived at the second robbery scene at Barclays Bank, Orange Grove, to carry out investigations.

It was to be a busy day for the crack squad.

The three armed gangsters entered the bank at 12.30 pm and took up their accustomed positions. Heyl at the door, McCall in the centre of the banking hall and Stander at the counter, gun in hand, went to the counter. 'This is a holdup,' he said.

Mrs Vivian King was joined at the counter by the second teller, Mrs Elaine O'Keefe, who did not realise what was happening.

'This is a holdup,' the robber repeated for her benefit.

Then notes of all denominations were passed over the counter and quickly stuffed into a bag.

One of the receptionists was on the telephone and one of the gunmen gesticulated for her to replace the receiver – which she did. Apart from the two tellers and the receptionist, no one else realised a robbery was going on.

The robbers then strolled down two flights of stairs and out to the getaway car.

Once the gang was clear of the banking hall, one of the employees rushed to a window and was in time to see the gang getting into their powder blue Ford Cortina.

The bank clerk was surprised to see the getaway car stop at a stop sign, wait for the cross traffic and then disappear.

While breaking most of the laws in the common law book, they very sensibly obeyed the statutory traffic laws as open violations would soon have drawn unwanted police attention.

It would be carelessness in this respect which would one day cost Stander his life.

By now media speculation that the bank hoppers were in fact André Stander and his henchmen was growing ever more persistent, but the Police refused to confirm this.

Thursday the 19th January brought the Stander gang a total haul of R167 000. But they decided to pull one more good job.

The target selected was the Barclays Bank in Isando, east of Johannesburg, the very next day. Stander had spent a long time casing this bank, believing it would bring them their largest bonus. It wasn't but the sum was still considerable.

The bank, in Electron Street, is situated between Johannesburg and Jan Smuts airport. Stander knew it well. It bordered on the area he covered as captain commanding the Criminal Investigation Department at Kempton Park.

Isando, like Wynberg, is an industrial suburb, but much bigger. Factories and office blocks, part of Johannesburg's eastern development plan, are situated only five kilometers from the international airport. The area is bisected by a highway and is near to a big interchange making it easy for a quick getaway.

They walked in at 10.00 am and ordered Mrs A Griffin

and Mr N Day to fill a bag with money.

They also took a gun from a security guard and another belonging to the bank.

This raid yielded R65 000.

But the gang was almost caught shortly after the robbery. On the highway heading back towards Johannesburg, their blue Ford Cortina XR-6 was spotted by two policemen in a prowl car.

Unfortunately, the policemen were travelling in the opposite direction. In spite of the wailing siren and flashing lights on the police car, oncoming traffic, particularly a large truck, blocked their efforts to immediately cross the traffic island and give chase. By the time they had turned it was too late: their quarry was gone.

Video Breakthrough

From this last robbery, however, the Police were able to positively identify the bank hoppers. Closed circuit video cameras, positioned strategically in the bank as part of the security system, produced photographs of the three men robbing the bank. The Bank made these available to the Police and they formed the package that was later handed to the Press for publication.

The bank predators had netted more than half a million rand in a series of dramatically outrageous raids in a mere five months.

And they had still not been caught. Their very success, however, had sown the seeds of a disastrous over confidence.

They had begun to make mistakes and the net had started to close.

7

The Lily Rose

January 1984

During the New Year the gang decided to take a three week break from crime and set about making arrangements to ensure their permanent freedom.

Stander drove to Cape Town in the now infamous stolen yellow Porsche Targa. He and Heyl, who followed separately in another vehicle, were all set to buy the fully equipped ocean going yacht, the *Lily Rose,* which was to cost them R219 000. A further R30 000 was used to purchase enough supplies to take the boat across the Atlantic.

The yacht was anchored at the staid and famous Royal Cape Yacht Club in Cape Town – the scene of the start to the Cape to Rio yacht races.

The *Lily Rose* typified Stander's eye for the good things in life. The fast, steel hulled yacht was the ultimate in luxurious cruising. The gang aimed to get it and probably some of their spoils to Fort Lauderdale in Miami, one of the best yacht basins in the world. It was well appointed as a starting point for a long holiday cruise in the Caribbean. Perhaps, after a good holiday, they would sell the boat and split the proceeds.

The nineteen ton *Lily Rose,* launched in 1981, was moored in Simonstown until it was moved to the Royal Cape Yacht

Club in October 1983. It sleeps nine people in two wood panelled state rooms and a big saloon. She has a 1850-litre fuel tank which gives her six cylinder one hundred and twenty horsepower diesel engine a two thousand nautical mile sailing range.

The yacht was built in Maitland by Bill Cooper, its former owner. Using nothing but the best materials, he took four years to build it. It was intended for his retirement. But the Stander gang bought it for use after their early retirement from bank hopping in South Africa.

After the Police located the *Lily Rose* it remained at Simonstown. Although it remained the property of Stander, McCall and Heyl, the banks have the right to sue the estates of the deceased members of the gang.

But, meanwhile, the luxury yacht still needed weekly maintenance. And as the legal issues would wrangle on for months and the condition of the boat could seriously deteriorate.

Stander had already been declared insolvent after his capture in 1980.

The cash for the purchase price of the yacht was legally held by Bill Cooper for he had sold the yacht in good faith.

Bill Cooper told of the events leading up to the sale of the *Lily Rose*.

'My broker, Ian Allen, and I were approached on 17th January by two very ordinary men who said they were interested in buying the *Lily Rose*. We arranged to meet them at the quayside where I unlocked the boat for them.'

Nothing Odd

'I met the two men. There was nothing odd about them. I did not suspect anything and as a result I do not remember very much about them,' said Bill Cooper after being informed of their true identities by the Police.

'You will get the money tomorrow,' André Stander said in a telephone call after deciding to buy the yacht. Stander took only an hour to make his decision.

Stander and Heyl concluded the deal, through Ian Allen, a yacht broker, the same day.

They wined and dined with their new sailing friends at the

Royal Cape Yacht Club and at the Cape Sun Hotel, where they were staying.

Stander wrote his address correctly as Number 5, Sixth Avenue, Houghton – where his partner McCall was fated to be shot dead – on the hotel's registration form.

Was this a similar arrogance to the instance where he hired a car in his own name to do a job and used his own Barclay Card to pay for it immediately prior to his first arrest, or was it a deliberate act to set up McCall? (Ironically, the Cape Sun had spent a small fortune on public relations by getting celebrities to visit the brand new luxury hotel. By accident, they achieved stunning publicity of an unwelcome nature.)

Stander and Heyl hired Ian Allen and Peter Hosford to sail the yacht to America. Besides McCall and Heyl, Allen had intended to take his family along as the crew. Hosford, a professional sailor who was formerly in the South African Navy, is well known in sailing circles in Cape Town. He was to co-skipper the *Lily Rose* with Allen.

In the beginning Hosford had been totally taken in by the disguises and arrogance of the two crooks. They were flashing large sums of money and talking big.

Acted Like a Poofter

Hosford described Stander as a 'hell of a nice guy'. He said Heyl had been 'dressed like a poofter' in 'tight black pants and a frilly shirt and had acted much too big for this boots'.

Hosford said that after the meeting he had joked with Royal Cape Yacht Club members that the men could be the hunted bank robbers. 'They were driving a yellow Porsche and this started the joking.'

Later, though, he became suspicious and telephoned the Camps Bay police. His suspicions had taken time to harden. His tip off was important but, according to police sources, the key to locating the yacht was information discovered at the house where McCall was shot.

Other important information had been painfully gathered in after extensive enquiries by Warrant Officer Jeff Benzine of the Cape Town Murder and Robbery Squad. He had been tipped off by a former fellow prisoner of Heyl's, now a Cape Town taxi driver, that he had twice seen Heyl riding a motor bike in the Peninsula. He had ridden down to Cape Town in it.

The bike, a 550cc Yamaha, was afterwards seized by police at Number 62, Houghton Drive.

The South African Railway Police, who control South Africa's harbours, took up position outside the harbour using their Boat Unit. Every craft passing out of the harbour was searched.

The gangsters arranged to pay for the yacht in full by depositing the purchase price directly into the Trust Bank account of Ian Allen, the yacht broker at Woodstock in the Cape and this they did. They would deposit various cash amounts and at various banks until it was paid for.

They had covered their debt with their robberies: their dream yacht was within their grasp.

Then, in early February, a team of detectives from Johannesburg, led by Brigadier Willem van der Merwe, and consisting of Major Gerrit Viljoen, Captain Johan Pretorius and Lieutenant Johan de Waal, swooped on the yacht club and seized the *Lily Rose*.

And thus the gang's plans were thrown into final disarray.

8

The Net Closes

For the next few weeks the gang went to ground. They spent the time arranging the bank drafts at various branches of Trust Bank in Johannesburg and living it up at the Houghton hideouts.

At about this time a man who identified himself as Frank called in at the Auto Bavaria showrooms in Rosebank and expressed interest in buying a luxury silver grey BMW sedan.

The salesman, Mr Robin Blake, was delighted.

Frank (who was later identified as McCall) said he was staying at his father's place in Houghton and was looking for a nice executive car for his wife. It would be a cash deal.

'We got into the car to take it for a test drive,' said Mr Blake. 'He looked a bit nervous but I didn't think much of it. He was driving and we went on the highway. Near the Wynberg/Sandton turnoff he stopped the car.

'He said that he wanted to get the feel of the car from the passenger's side because his wife was very fussy. We both started to get out of the car, but as soon as I turned my back he jumped back in and sped off.'

This vehicle was destined to be the last one McCall was to drive in his life.

The South African Police were in the meantime meticu

lously gathering in segments of the vital information which, when pieced together, would spell the end of the runaway crime marathon.

On Monday the 23rd January information was leaked to the Press that police were in possession of video film of all three members of the Stander gang taken while they were robbing one of the Barclays banks.

Video Information

The information was used without consulting the Police and they were furious.

They accused the Press of hampering their investigations. They had not wanted the Stander gang, or any other bank robbers for that matter, to become aware what countermeasures were in existence.

The Press, as a result, were asked not to refer to video cameras installed in banks in the future.

Nevertheless, the fact remains that the Police were in possession of vital photographic shots which would likely bring them immediate results if they were flashed on television or shown in the newspapers.

The Police still had a problem though. The pictures taken during the course of a robbery are valuable evidence for production at any later trial. This value would be lessened if they were released, as a court would likely hold that this had prejudiced the accused persons' case.

It was a difficult decision.

At a special press conference on Thursday the 26th January, the head and shoulder pictures of the three gang members were released. They received instant wide coverage in the news media and on television.

Police were later to say that although they were already in possession of vital evidence which led to the later breakthroughs, the publication of the gang's pictures did play an important role in their investigations.

Edenvale Bonus

During January the police put a large number of men on special duty, working in pairs in and around banks on the Reef.

They were armed and ready and waiting for the bank hoppers to strike. They had walki-talki radios, too, to call for assistance immediately they came up against something.

The extra precautions didn't net the police the bank hoppers, but their efforts did not pass unrewarded.

On Thursday the 26th January 1984 four black men walked into the Volkskas Bank in Eden Centre, Van Riebeeck Street, Edenvale, and approached the security guard, Eric van Greunen, and asked to use the telephone.

'I told them to go to the other side,' said Mr van Greunen.

He then went on to say how they produced weapons. Two had handguns, one a sawn off shotgun and the other a panga.

One relieved the security guard of his gun and the robbers then held up the staff and told them all to go into the strongroom.

The manager, Mr Gideon du Plessis, was speaking to his wife on the telephone and he asked her to call the Police.

Then, two East Rand policemen on the lookout for the Stander gang, Constable A J Kruger and Warrant Officer J L Steyn got to the bank as the robbers were leaving.

They surprised the policemen and disarmed them, then forced them back into the bank.

The raiders then ran out of the bank again, this time to find themselves up against Constable Giyane who was on routine beat duty. He opened fire and shot one of the gangsters in the head, killing him outright.

The bandit returned fire and Constable Giyane went down with a bullet in his leg.

The three remaining gang members leapt into a waiting van and drove away in a hurry, knocking down a pedestrian and side swiping several cars in the process.

Constable Giyane, not a man who gave up easily, fired again from his prone position on the street and one of his bullets hit the driver of the getaway car in his back.

Warrant Officer Steyn and Constable Kruger, having rearmed themselves, gave chase in a car, caught up and after several shots forced them off the road.

The driver was shot again during the chase and died shortly afterwards.

The surviving two robbers were arrested and R90 000 in

cash was recovered from the van.

During the shootout stray bullets were fired into the Life Book Room bookshop opposite the bank.

One bullet went through the hair of an assistant, Mrs Watermeyer, skimmed the cheek and nicked the ear of Minister's wife, Mrs E van Rooyen, and buried itself in a Bible stored in a back storeroom.

The publication of the bank video pictures had brought instant results.

Information began pouring in – a lot of it apparently from escort agency women who the gang had taken to their hideouts.

Police were simultaneously passed information about two of the fugitives' hideouts, Number 5, Sixth Avenue, Lower Houghton and the other at Number 7, Nina Street, Linmeyer.

On Friday the 27th January Stander told Mr Alfred Gumani, the African gardener at the Houghton hideout, that he was going on holiday to the Drakensberg, although he was in fact on his way to the United States.

McCall, who normally stayed at Number 7, Nina Street, Linmeyer, moved in and lived there on his own. The move would cost him his life.

Heyl was staying at another rented hideout at Number 62, Houghton Drive, until the time came for him and McCall to sail for America in the *Lily Rose,* which was scheduled to leave Cape Town on Saturday the 11th February.

Besides these three luxury hideouts it is possible that they had others.

The *modus operandi* was for each gang member to stay for most of the time in separate houses, for reasons of security. But they would visit each other to plan, have parties or watch videos.

Houghton Stake-out

On Saturday the 28th January at 5.30 pm members of Police Johannesburg's crack Reaction Unit took up observation at Number 5, Sixth Avenue, Houghton, north of the city centre and at Number 7, Nina Street, Linmeyer.

The Reaction Unit of the South African Police was

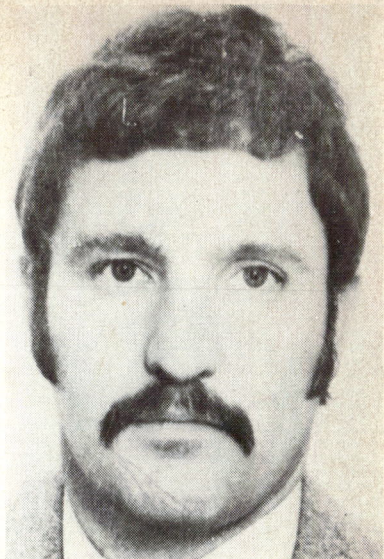

The Many Faces of Stander

1 Rugby Player (above)　　　　　2 Policeman (above)

3 Convicted robber (below)　　　　4 Fugitive (below)

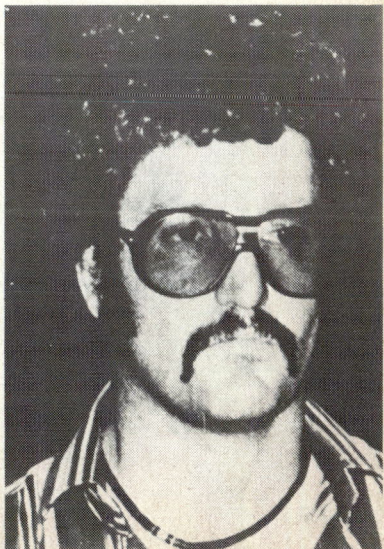

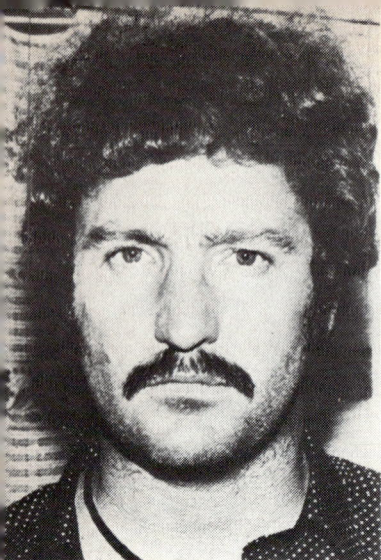

More Faces of Stander

5 Fugitive   6 Caught by a Bank Camera

7 Gen. Frans Stander Mourns his son (below)

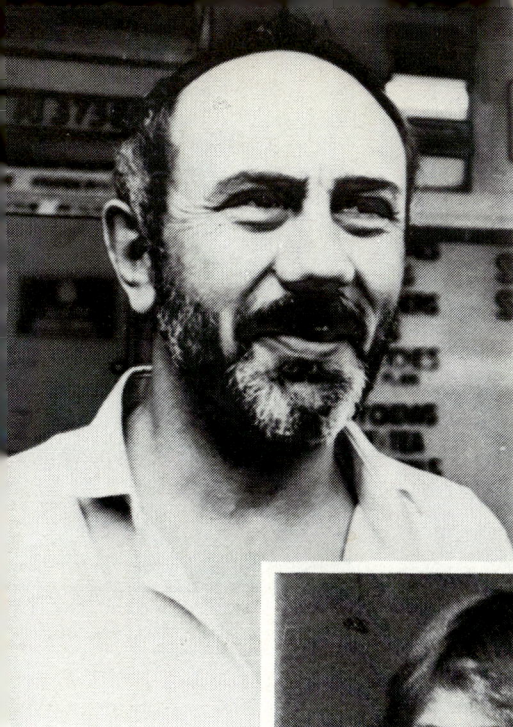
8 His former friend, Cor van Deventer

9 His ex-wife, Bekkie

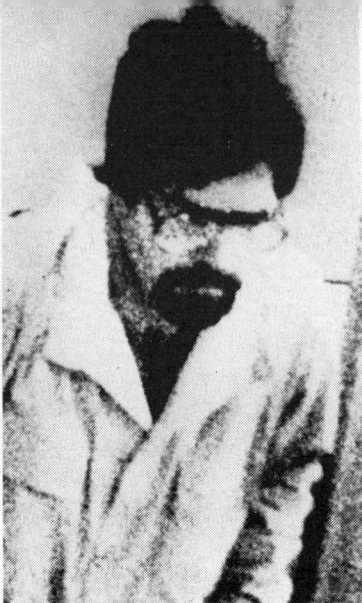

10 Allan George Heyl – caught by a bank camera (above)

11 Patrick Leigh McCall – caught by a bank camera (above)

12 Heyl – another face (below)

13 McCall – another face (below)

14 (Top) **The 'A' Team**
(L/R) Brig M van der
Linde, Chief Brixton
Murder and Robbery
Squad, Gen. C.
Zietsman, OC CID
RSA, Maj. L.
Neethling, OC
Police Forensic
Laboratories and
Brig. Kierie Spies,
OC CID
Witwatersrand

15 (Right) A false alarm
in Pretoria

16 (Top) 'They went thataway'
– Mr A Hornby outside the
workshop at Olifantsfontein
from where the gang
'sprang' Heyl

17 (Right) Mrs Barkhuizen
displays the gangsters' taste
in videos

18 Strongroom at the Pot Shot gunshop where McCall gunned down Mrs Malene Henn. Note blood stains on boxes

The Heroines – the Girls who fought back

19 Mrs Malene Henn (right)

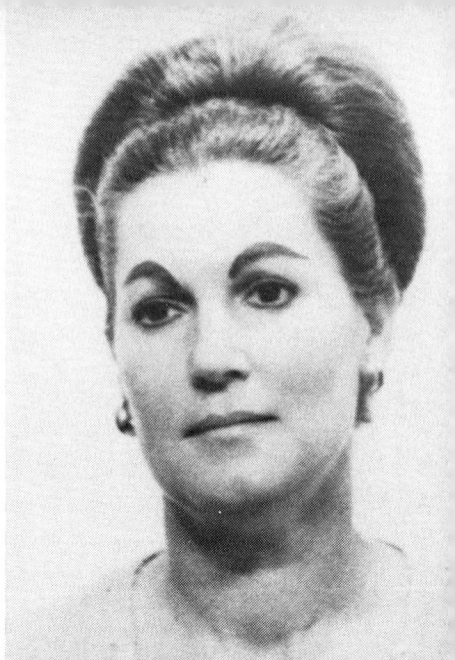

20 (Below) Mrs. Remona van Staden standing by the car robbed from her by Stander and later wrecked

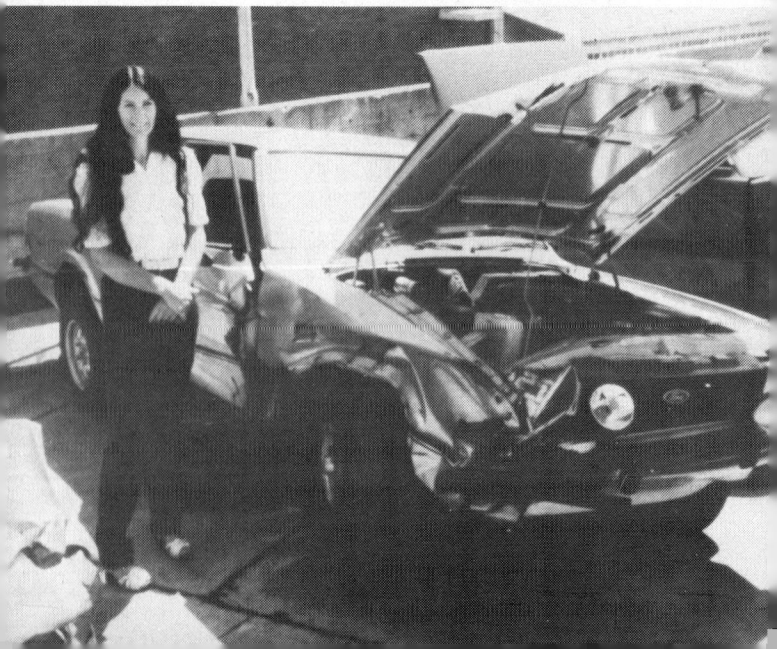

21 Patrick Leigh McCall
died here

22 The owner of 5 Sixth
Ave, Houghton, Mr
Peter Snyman,
unhappily surveys
the wreckage after
the shootout

23 The shootout house

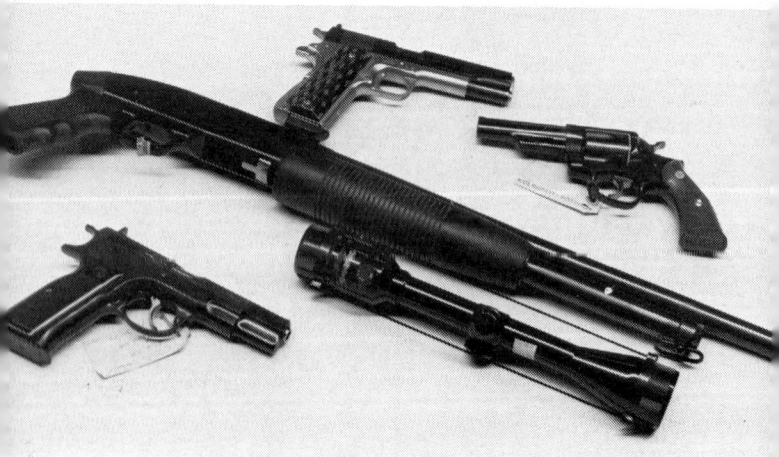

24 Stolen guns recovered by Police

Other Hideouts

25 62 Houghton Drive (Top)   26 7 Nina Street, Linmeyer (bottom)

Steals on Wheels

27 That canary yellow Porche Targa (top)

28 That getaway car – the XR-6 Ford Cortina Interceptor (bottom)

29 The dreamboat – Lily
Rose

30 The dream shattered
(right)

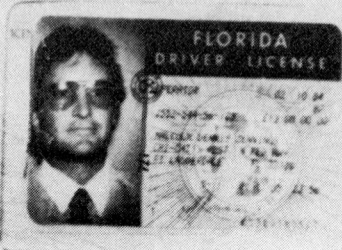

31 The last faces of Stander (top)

32 The face of reality – crime didn't pay (below)

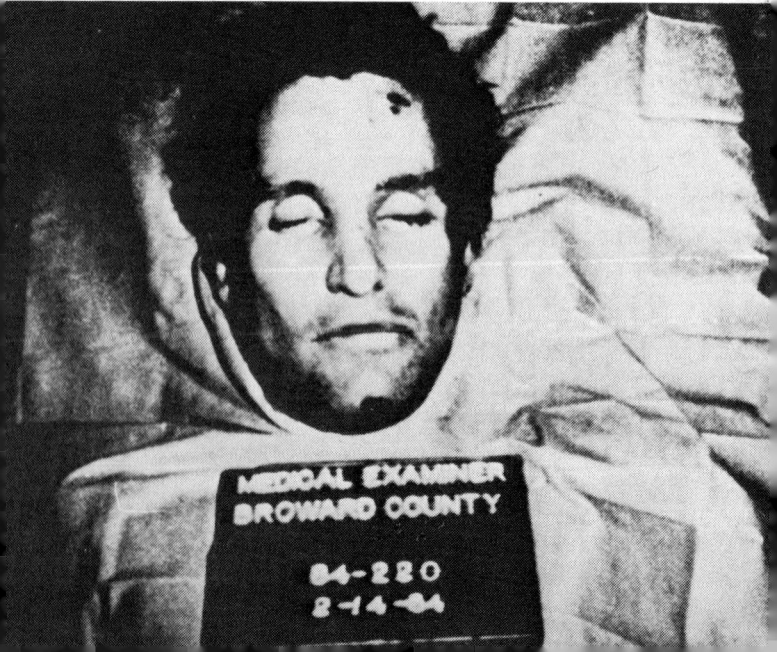

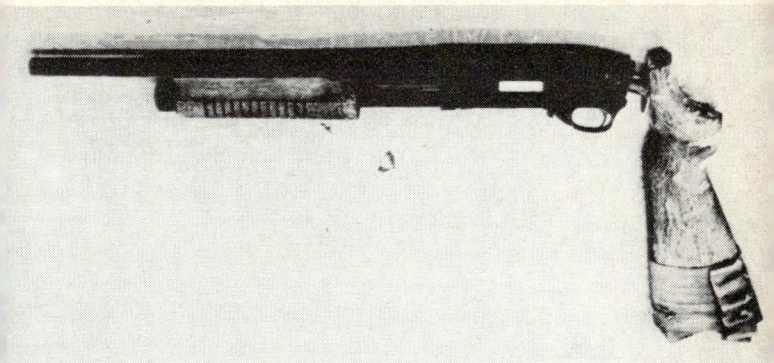

33 (Top) Shotgun broken in Stander's last desperate struggle with Officer von Stetina in Fort Lauderdale before he was shot dead

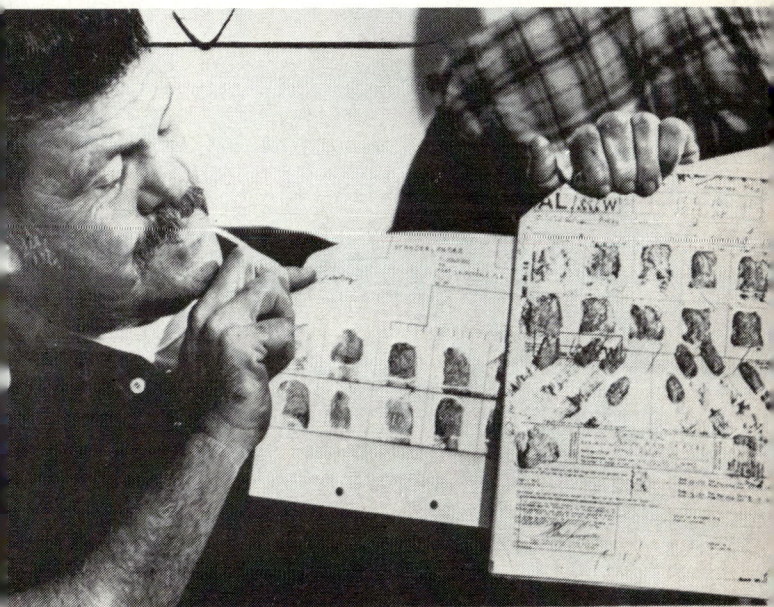

34 (Below) He's dead and that's official. Fort Lauderdale detective, Tac Cone, confirms the fingerprint identification

Sunday Times
THE PAPER FOR THE PEOPLE
FEBRUARY 19 1984
PRICE 50c incl. Tax

The last moments

STANDER'S END

A cop watches as he dies in the dirt

By PATRICK CHENEY and NEIL HOOPER

THIS was the end of the road for Andre Stander.

35 The Sunday Times front page of February 19th 1984, says it all

formed during the 1976 unrest in the black townships around the country. Initially called the Riot Squad, it is specifically designed to quell any urban unrest.

The name was changed to the Reaction Unit in 1982.

During comparatively quiet times the men attached to the Unit are deployed to perform in almost any police duty – roadblocks, stake-outs and general undercover police work.

They operate in both camouflage uniform and plain clothes, rarely in the traditional blue police gear. These highly trained professionals are well able to handle any danger situation.

They believed they had made their first real break-through in the six month hunt for the Stander gang. Other policemen were posted in adjacent houses belonging to various mystified neighbours, but none of them were en-lightened as to exactly what the Police were looking for.

The members of the Reaction Unit were in radio contact with each other.

The Police had received positive information that the gang had rented the houses.

Right Psychological Spot

The neighbours of Number 5, Sixth Avenue, had certainly not suspected anything amiss or unusual when various luxury cars had been parked in the drive. After all, everyone in Hou-ghton drives a fancy car.

So clearly they had hit the right psychological spot when they chose Houghton as a place for rich outlaws to hide.

The African maid kept the house tidy and the African gar-dener ensured that the lawns were regularly trimmed. There were no suspicions aroused because the tenants hardly used the pool or tennis court of the rented R1 600 a month home. People in Houghton tend to keep themselves to themselves. It is a neighbourhood of successful businessmen, ambassa-dors and politicians. The wealthy and successful value their privacy.

The gang members affected the same affluent private school manner, so they fitted in well.

From across the street, in a front room used as an obser-vation post, police identified two stolen cars in the drive way. One of them was the by now infamous blue Ford Cortina Intercepter XR-6, which was believed to have been used as a getaway car in at least ten holdups. It had originally been white, but had been resprayed blue in a hurry, even the adhesive stripes along the sides had been oversprayed. This confirmed they were hot on the trail.

It was now only a matter of time before an arrest was made.

The Police maintained their vigils throughout the night. There was no movement on the premises. Everything looked normal. Throughout the whole of Sunday the police waited anxiously, monitoring every movement in the quiet streets and radioing it to the headquarters of the hunt at Brixton.

On Sunday 29th January at 11.30 pm a silver grey BMW turned into Sixth Avenue. It was the one stolen from Auto Bavaria in Rosebank. Its slow progression down the avenue was noted by the watching officers. It turned into the driveway of Number 5.

Only one man was inside and he got out.

The watchers immediately identified him as Stander's lieutenant, Patrick Leigh McCall.

He was known as the mystery man of the gang. Little was openly known of him, although he had a criminal record dating back to 1969 when, at the age of twenty, he had been convicted of theft and gaoled for three years.

Waiting Game

The Police did not make a move but continued to wait and watch. They didn't wish to make their move precipitiously as they felt pretty sure Stander and the other gang member, Allan Heyl, were either present already, or would be coming there soon.

Throughout the early hours of the 30th January the Police waited and watched.

A decision was made to bring the Special Task Force to Houghton. It was on immediate standby in Pretoria some fifty kilometers away.

The Police Special Task Force is an elite SWAT (Special Weapons and Tactics Team) unit formed after the Fox Street siege of the Israeli Consulate in Johannesburg in 1975.

Security of personnel and operations is paramount. The

114

members of the unit are anonymous like the crack British Special Air Service and the German GSG9 group. Its commander is Brigadier Bert Wandrag, who took charge of the the Silverton bank siege.

'I don't like any publicity, the fewer people who know about us the better,' the Brigadier said recently.

His men are hand picked. They train in numerous skills ranging from mountaineering to scuba diving. Some of the Special Task Force men dived to rescue victims of the recent Laingsberg floods.

'I'm not interested in men who are just physically strong. Give me a man who has a strong personality and I'll make him into a tiger.'

He took personal charge of the Unit at Houghton; his tigers were about to maul the Stander gang.

The Hunt Begins

Senior detectives left their offices at John Vorster Square, Johannesburg's Police Headquarters, and joined the Murder and Robbery Squad at the stake-out.

Sixth Avenue was cordoned off shortly before 5.00 am. Sharpshooters from the Police Special Task Force moved into positions at the front of the house, in the adjoining gardens and in the pool area of the Greek Consulate which backed on to the Stander hideout.

The two suburban blocks in the neighbourhood came to a complete standstill. Home owners were woken up and warned to stay inside their houses, to keep away from the windows and to remain low in case of flying bullets.

Direct Assault

Shortly before dawn police officers with megaphones set the whole thing in motion.

'It's the Police. Come out with your hands above your head. The place is surrounded!'

McCall's reaction was immediately positive and Police ducked for cover as the desperate and crazed McCall opened fire on them from inside the house.

'Go to hell, come in and get me,' McCall screamed out while running from window to window firing wildly.

The Police returned fire with R-4 carbines, automatic

shot guns and handguns. Members of the Unit finally crept forward and lobbed two grenades into a smashed bedroom window.

Afterwards, in a direct assault, police burst through the broken windows and spread out inside.

McCall was dead, shot in the neck and side.

A policeman said it looked as if he had been trying to climb up into the roof.

A bloodied pillow lay near his body. The body of one of the country's most hunted criminals.

It has been a subject of conjecture, however, that during the last stages of the siege, McCall took his own life by putting the gun in his mouth and pulling the trigger.

The house was found to be riddled with bullet holes as the detectives and Special Task Force men checked it out.

One policeman had been wounded in McCall's last ditch stand. He was Sergeant J D Jonge who had a bullet wound in his forearm.

Sound and Fury

There had been much sound and fury that memorable day in Houghton.

A doctor living in Central Street, near the scene of the drama, said: 'The Police handled the matter exceptionally well. There was no wild shooting from their side but the guy in the house went crazy, firing a lot of shots.'

General Zietsman laconically described the scene 'as a small Beirut in Lower Houghton'.

In the house the Police recovered a veritable arsenal of weapons. There was a total of one thousand four hundred rounds of ammunition, a shotgun and eight handguns.

As well as this, but of greater pecuniary interest to the lemon-mouthed Clearing Bankers' Association, they only found cash amounting to R5 000.

They also discovered evidence of the high life style of the gang. There was expensive imported liquor, including German, Dutch and French champagne. Caviar and Italian ice cream were in the fridge.

Dusty amid the rubble was a pile of motoring magazines, including one in which an article described the peak road performance of the Cortina XR-6 Interceptor.

There were women's magazines, too, scattered about the house as well as cosmetics in one of the bathrooms, so the bank hoppers had not been short of female company.

One of the front rooms had a neat trap door cut in the floor boards, which probably had been used to stash the stolen money. Nearby this trap was a calculating machine on a table, against which were three chairs. Unlike the rest of the house, which was neat and conservative, girlie photos were pasted on the walls of this room.

From Three to Two

The Police had hit one of the gang's main hideouts and recovered some loot and guns. That had to be a big blow to the gang. McCall was dead; the central three had become two again.

McCall's brother, Peter McCall, a professional man in Johannesburg, commented that the prison system had not 'reformed him (McCall) but humiliated him'.

His brother had been determined not to go back to gaol, even at the cost of killing himself. 'But the fact that he fought back, even when he realised it was all over, says so much about the person he really was.'

When McCall's victim, Malene Henn, the gun shop proprietor, heard of his death, she said: 'It is sad that someone should die this way.'

Although Mrs Henn has been told by doctors that it would take her at least six months to fully recover, she said: 'I know he tried to kill me, but I don't feel happy about his death!'

An old friend said McCall was known as a tough in his school days. 'He was smaller than most guys but always getting into fights. In spite of that he hardly ever lost one.'

Other school mates who attended Lyttleton Manor High School in Pretoria with him said that, although he was naughty, he was a loyal friend.

During the search of the premises afterwards, police burst into the room of Alfred Gumani, the gardener at the hideout.

'Who lives in this house?' a policeman asked the gardener.

'Mr Grey arrived here on Friday,' the shocked gardener replied.

Never Steal

Stander, McCall and Heyl had all resorted to aliases. Stander used the name Mark Jennings, McCall became Peter Grey and Heyl adopted the name of Kenny Roberts.

The owners of the rented house knew them by those names – and never suspected they were pseudonyms.

The African gardener liked and respected Stander, who had the hardnecked effrontery once to say to Mr Gumani: 'Never steal – always work for your money.'

This police victory marked the beginning of the end for André Stander. Tell tale leads, including an address in Fort Lauderdale found in the house, would eventually cause his downfall.

But, while the Police had gained their first major break-through at Number 5, Sixth Avenue, Houghton and were observing at Number 7, Nina Street, Linmeyer, yet another luxury house had been rented by the gang. The pictures of the three men flashed in the Press and on television finally led police to this hideout.

A reporter from *The Star*, Trevor Jones, was hot on the trail as well. He got the Linmeyer address from the Southern Suburbs Video Shop where Stander had once again carelessly given an accurate address.

Not expecting it to be correct, Trevor Jones went ahead of his photographer and walked up to the door, knocked and was immediately grabbed by a burly policeman in plain clothes who presumed he was a member of the Stander gang.

The owner of the house is Mrs Jenny Peters. She was full of praise for the gang: 'They turned out to be perfect tenants. If I ever came to the house, they helped me carry anything I wanted to the car and even opened the door for me.'

In conversations they told Mrs Peters that they were in electronics. McCall, she said, had a leg in plaster and his jaw wired up. 'One thing I noticed about Jennings (Stander) is that he kept changing the colour of his hair to various shades of blonde. He had no moustache and looked completely different in the picture released by the Police.'

The maid at the house said that two girls visited and stayed over a few times. One was a blonde and the other was a brunette accompanied by a small boy.

Whoever these girls were, it was a risky breach of security. Added to this, it was later established that the gang used the services of escort agencies, some of them to supply high class prostitutes.

Never Trust Anyone

McCall told Jenny Peters that they were pulling out to open a new branch of their business in Harare.

'Never trust anyone like you trusted us again,' he said to her before he left.

Immediately after the McCall shootout, as a result of information found at the house, police set up surveillance at another luxury house – Number 62, Houghton Drive, only seven blocks from where McCall was shot.

In the driveway was the stolen canary yellow Porsche convertible, two other vehicles and a motorbike. The bike, a Yamaha 550 cc, and one of the vehicles, an off-road four wheeled drive Suzuki, had been bought by the gang during their spending spree. Heyl was a bike fanatic.

They had found three two-way radios with indications that attempts had been made to tune one of them to the police frequencies but this had failed due to the lack of a second crystal.

Another arsenal of weapons was also seized.

Afterwards the Police took up positions in and around the four hundred thousand rand house and kept surveillance until the 6th February before they finally concluded they were wasting their time. The birds had flown.

Stander was in America and Heyl had panicked and fled after the Houghton shootout.

No one knows where he is, although the Police believe he escaped overseas.

They knew he took Stander to Jan Smuts airport to catch his plane on the 27th January but after that there was no further trace, except that the silver grey BMW, stolen from Auto Bavaria in Rosebank about ten days before, was abandoned in Pretoria on the 30th January, presumably after the news of the Houghton shootout and McCall's death broke.

Heyl was and is running scared, but where he ran to and where he is running now is still unknown.

The circumstances surrounding the leasing of this third hideout was example of the gang's arrogance.

Towards the end of 1983 the owner of the house, Johannesburg businessman Mr Raymond Matuson, put the house on the books of an estate agency and asked them to find a tenant.

Charming Gentlemen

The Italian Trade Commissioner in South Africa had already shown interest in renting the property, when a Mr Clayton (they had obviously had too much of a diet of Dallas) was introduced as a possible tenant by the agency.

Two 'charming gentlemen' arrived at the Houghton Drive house and introduced themselves to Mr Matuson as Clayton (Stander) and Kenny (Heyl). Their facial expressions didn't even twitch when they were told the rent was two thousand rand per month, which even by rich South African standards is regarded as exceptionally high.

Ray Matuson is a shrewd businessman. He told the potential tenants to meet his lawyer and conclude a formal deal. They agreed and a meeting was set up at the city centre offices of his lawyer. All this time pictures of the three convicts had been flashed on television and had appeared constantly in the daily and Sunday Press. Still no one suspected the two gentlemen bandits.

Stander and Heyl sat face to face across a desk with the attorney and the owner of the house. Stander signed the lease agreement using his false name and concluded the deal with a deposit of R4 000 in cash which he paid into Ray Matuson's bank account.

Matuson was dismayed when the Police approached him and advised him that his house had been used as a secret hideout by the Stander gang.

'Mr Clayton (Stander) struck me as a charming young man. He was a tall, good looking man with brown hair and a moustache. He spoke of the action he had seen while fighting in Rhodesia and of the death amongst his friends.'

According to Mr Matuson, both Kenny and Clayton 'were happily divorced, and spoke of the high divorce rate in Zimbabwe'.

It should be noted here that the gang stole the passport of Brian Kenny when they raided the Volkskas Bank at Jan Smuts Airport on the 4th December.

Red Herrings

The references to Harare were clearly red herrings. Stander had no intention of heading for Zimbabwe, but for the United States.

Three days before McCall's death, on the 27th January, Stander flew to America. He bought the ticket in one of Johannesburg's busiest travel agencies, and drew the maximum foreign exchange allowance of six thousand rand in dollars. The ticket he bought was routed Johannesburg – New York, with a connecting flight to Fort Lauderdale aboard Delta Airlines flight DL 1051 on 28th January. At the last minute he changed his flight and travelled via Rio de Janeiro.

To buy his initial ticket Stander used a passport in the name of Malcolm Dennis Jennings.

On the 20th November 1983 Stander had called at the Kempton Park home of Mr and Mrs Malcolm Jennings. He introduced himself as Sergeant Venter and said he was investigating a fraud. Stander later arranged to collect Mr Jennings' passport after showing police accreditation and it was this he used to get out of the country.

Stander clearly thought he had run rings around his former colleagues of the South African Police and this did nothing to diminish his arrogance. But in America Stander was to find himself playing in a new and completely unfamiliar ball game.

9

Flight to America

January – February 1984

On Friday the 27th January André Stander fled to America. It will never be known whether he intended to make the big crime league there, or whether he wanted to retire and slip into obscurity.

He was to find himself a small fish in a very large sea. Things were different. He had to deal with people he did not understand and who thought his accent strange. Suddenly he stood out.

The Police Force worked differently, too, and he was obviously unfamiliar with their methods.

Fort Lauderdale is a tough place, a haven for drug smugglers and general rogues. It is the gateway to Cuba and the Caribbean and has a very big yacht basin and consequently a large transient population.

Stander had arrived in the hot and steamy south Florida town on the 2nd February. He was on his own – without his henchmen Patrick McCall and Allan Heyl – and he had to fend for himself.

In Fort Lauderdale the local police – highly regarded in American Police circles – and the FBI – the Federal Bureau of Investigation – were all set to arrest him. But they knew very little about South Africa's most wanted man and because of his passion for disguise it was extremely difficult to identify him.

The biggest mistake Stander had made up until then was to leave clues in the Houghton hideout which, when passed on by the South Africans, would lead the Fort Lauderdale Police to an address in the town.

Urgent liaison had been established by the South African Police with their American counterparts, through the Federal Bureau of Investigation and the respective departments of foreign affairs.

The yacht, the *Lily Rose,* was another clue which led to Stander's downfall. The boat was to sail for Fort Lauderdale where they probably intended to sell it eventually. The proceeds would have given Stander and his gang a stake to start a new life.

When it was seized in Cape Town the Police were informed by the skipper that the *Lily Rose* had been due to set sail for Fort Lauderdale on the 11th February.

Stander was never again to see the ocean going yacht he had so carefully planned for and set up.

Pure Speculation

The Police, though, refused to say too much to the Press, presumably in case it hampered their investigations. They said the theory that Stander was heading for Fort Lauderdale was 'pure speculation'.

Some senior police officials said that it was assumed Stander was still in South Africa and that investigations into his whereabouts were continuing.

Up until four days before Stander's end, the Florida police denied they were involved in any hunt for the fugitive.

'We have heard all about André Stander because we have been plagued by telephone calls from South African journalists. But we have received no official orders to track down South Africa's most wanted man,' the Florida Police said on Thursday the 9th February.

South African Police had, though, already sent the Federal Bureau of Investigation information regarding the fugitive.

Meanwhile, in the United States, Stander was using an assumed name. The surname he was using happened to match the name of the street in which his father lived in Pretoria – Harris Street – but his reason for using the name was a different one. He was carrying the passport of Peter Harris that he had stolen during the course of the robbery at Volkskas Bank at Jan Smuts airport on the night of Sunday the 4th December.

Pink Pussycat

On his arrival in Fort Lauderdale, Stander moved into the apartment he had leased while still in Johannesburg but he only stayed there a short time.

He quickly rented another apartment at $333 per month in north west Fort Lauderdale.

There he met his next door neighbour, Miss Ayten Kiles, a stripper at the local night club, the Pink Pussycat, not far from the apartment block.

One night the big bosomed Miss Kiles had bumped into Stander when he was coming out of his flat shortly before 7.00 pm.

'Hi, I'm your new neighbour. How about having dinner with me tonight? I don't feel like dining alone,' Stander said.

Miss Kiles accepted.

'He seemed like a nervous guy. He was kind of jumpy,' she said.

Stander told her he had money tied up in his own country, but they would not let him take it out. He said he did not like it where he came from, but never told exactly where that place was. But, he told Ayten Kiles, he did not have to work. He had enough money to see him through. They had dinner, but not sex, the stripper explained afterwards.

Other people who noticed him at the apartment block mentioned that he had kept very much to himself and never received visitors.

He was often seen walking in the neighbourhood.

Australian Author

A writer in a local Fort Lauderdale newspaper described

the area as a transient city where lots of people move in and out constantly.

Stander was one of those many transients.

Not many people took much notice of him although a few of them might have read of Stander's exploits in South Africa and that he was believed to be in Fort Lauderdale. Stander passed himself off as an Australian author and people believed him. It was not unnatural to find someone in the city with a British or Australian accent.

Most of the crime centered around Fort Lauderdale is reputed to be drug related. The city proper comprises a number of small cities and has a population of about a million. Many of the people there are retired and living in condominiums.

Stander's flat was about two kilometers from the sea in an area with many rented apartment blocks and small motels. The rent he paid for his apartment was lower than average.

In the 1960s Fort Lauderdale was seen as a fun place where young people gathered during their summer vacations. An early movie entitled *Where the Boys Are,* which was shot in Fort Lauderdale, may have influenced Stander to seek refuge there.

Monumental Blunder

Thursday 9th February, the day the Fort Lauderdale Police denied they were hunting him, Stander made another monumental blunder.

He was driving a 1973 red Ford Mustang which he had bought in the city, when he was stopped by police officer, Larry Keesling, for driving an unregistered vehicle.

He was arrested and placed in the Fort Lauderdale police cells while bail was arranged.

Stander identified himself as Peter Harris. In compliance with local police routine Stander was stood against a wall and mug shots – both full face and side – were taken.

He was then given a a criminal number, something unheard of in traffic violation cases in South Africa. They also took his fingerprints before finally releasing him on a bail surety of one hundred dollars.

When stopped for the traffic violation, he told Officer Keesling that his name was Peter Harris and he was Australian. Yet he was carrying a British passport in the name of Bryan Kenny and the photograph on it matched him. The passport had also been stolen by Stander in the raid on the Volkskas Bank at Jan Smuts airport along with the Harris passport. This aroused the suspicions of the arresting officer but clearly not seriously.

As the face on the passport photograph appeared to be the same as Stander, he wasn't, fortunately for him, arrested and charged for a false passport violation.

Stopped by a Robot

The final charges brought against Stander were: failing to stop at a traffic light, driving an unregistered vehicle and failing to produce a driver's licence on demand. The fine for those offences was $200 but because Stander (or Harris as he was known to the police authorities) had a total of $5 600 in his possession, he was only required to pay a surety of $100.

He was set free as soon as the formalities regarding his photographing and fingerprints had been sorted out.

However, his red Mustang was put in the police pound for further checking because it carried illegal number plates.

In the State of Florida, as it is in most places, it is an offence to give a police officer a false name and yet they never charged him for this. In fact, it was only later after his release, that the Police suddenly became interested in the Stander case. This was because they had been contacted by the South African Police and given formal information, pictures and details of the various disguises of South Africa's most wanted man.

André Stander's case in all the steps along the way can best be described in one word – bizarre.

Here are the events which led up to the fateful day of his death:

• Friday the 27th January 1984. A man whose passport identified him as Malcolm Dennis Jennings arrived in New York city, only three days after obtaining an immigration

visa at the American consulate in Johannesburg.
• Thursday the 2nd February 1984 a man calling himself Mark Jennings flew to Fort Lauderdale aboard Delta Airlines and moved into a flat there.
• Thursday the 9th February 1984 a man, claiming to be a Peter Harris of Australia but carrying a British passport in the name of Bryan Kenny, was arrested by the Fort Lauderdale Police for traffic violations and then released on bail.

The same evening after his arrest and his car had been impounded, Stander went to see Anthony Tomasello, from whom he'd bought the Mustang, at his Chevron Service Station and asked to borrow his car.

'I've got a very important meeting at Shooters (a local nightspot) at six o'clock and I can't miss it,' Stander said.

When the car was returned the next day Tomasello recalled that it was full of sand and had used a full tank of petrol – enough to travel at least two hundred and fifty kilometers.

That morning, Friday the 10th February, in a desperate attempt to extricate himself from the mess he had found himself in, Stander firmed on his Jennings identity and went out and obtained a Florida driver's licence.

Idiotic Move

Then in a frankly idiotic move he went and stole his red Mustang back from the police pound. Clearly, he would have been better advised to have left it where it was and cleared town, but he didn't. This is particularly evident when it is appreciated that his car now had no number plates at all – not even false ones.

Detective Don Stevenson, a member of the auto theft squad, said he was at the pound making a routine check of the impounded vehicles, when he felt a tap on his shoulder.

It was Stander.

He asked if his car was ready to go.

Detective Stevenson told him to wait until he had finished his rounds, but when he returned both Stander and his car had gone.

'It gets very busy around here. Obviously nobody noticed him taking it out,' the detective said.

It was clear, however, that Stander's car had to be on the police wanted list, so he returned with it to Tomasello on Monday the 13th February.

When he dropped in, thirty three year old Mr Tomasello had been reading about Stander in the Fort Lauderdale *Sun Sentinel* - then the man himself appeared.

Mr Tomasello admits he was terrified.

'Just as I dropped the article, he walked into my office. His eyes bounced off the paper and looked right at me. By the look on his face, I could tell he had read it.

'He knew I was the only person who could identify him.'

Stander told Tomasello to go out to the back of the garage. The car needed some work on it, he said. As they went out, the garage owner suddenly became nervous.

'It occurred to me as we went, why the back?'

Tomasello spun around, pointed to the newspaper and demanded: 'Is this you?'

Stander replied: 'I can't believe they have caught up to me so quickly and they got the yacht as well.'

He then ordered Mr Tomasello to get the Mustang repainted as quickly as possible.

'I told him I'd do it. I knew an overnight paint place.' he said.

'I'll be back to take care of you later,' said Stander as he disappeared.

The petrified garage owner knew now that South Africa's most wanted criminal lived only a block away from his home, from his two young children and a pregnant wife.

He went to his lawyer, Mr Arne Colson, who immediately notified the Police and the Federal Bureau of Investigation. They urged that his wife and children leave town immediately, and advised Mr Tomasello not to go home himself.

After leaving Tomasello Stander went directly to a gun shop where he bought his last gun, a .38 Colt Python.

Presumably Stander, with his police experience, was of the opinion that second hand car dealers do not very readily have much to do with police. And, if Tomasello did, then a disguised threat would be enough to put him off his duty as a citizen.

But he was wrong: a petrified Tomasello contacted the Police because he believed that Stander was going to kill him.

A Few Hours to Live

Fort Lauderdale police together with the Federal Bureau of Investigation, now in possession of the vital information they needed to arrest the South African fugitive, began planning their strategy.

They had also, for reasons of their own previous arrest, been trying to find 'Jennings' but they had had trouble finding the right address.

Mr Tomasello put them right.

Members of their Tactical Impact Unit – the equivalent of the South African Police Special Task Force – were called in and Tomasello was asked to join them.

Stander seemed to be losing his grip.

He had gone through a red light, hardly a way to keep a low profile. He stole the Mustang back from the police pound and then took it back to the garage where he had bought it to get a respray.

He hadn't left town when he could and now he was up against the crack Tactical Impact Force, which is reputed to have a ninety five percent success rate on specific assignments. The local unit, much feared by criminals, is headed by Captain Ed White, and concentrates on armed robbery and burglary. It is made up of fourteen officers, two sergeants and Captain White.

During the ten years of its existence, the unit has not lost a single policeman.

'Every month my men have to take a fitness test and on top of this they must have a high degree of marksmanship,' Captain White explained.

Hazardous Duty

Although the unit concentrates on street crime, it is also called upon to cope with all manner of hazardous duty. This includes SWAT, general surveillance and the protection of VIPs.

In Stander's case the unit's brief was to commence observations at the address in their possession and watch out for the man they believed to be André Stander.

Stander, of course, was completely unaware of the latest police operation to apprehend him.

The ring was beginning to close around the cool bank robber, frustrated yachtsman and early day jetsetter.

As in South Africa, Stander still remained the fitness fanatic. In Johannesburg, according to his girlfriend Sue Hewitt, he ran about ten kilometers every morning from the first Houghton hideout.

He kept himself in perfect physical shape for any eventuality he might have to face, but this didn't help him in the end.

Stander had bought himself a racing bicycle and taken up regular training to keep himself fit.

Fort Lauderdale police had been informed of the purchase of the two wheeler and knew the exact description.

The South African Police had been told, too, by an informer and passed it on, but it is likely it was the same informer.

Final Stakeout

For several hours, the seven man team of the Tactical Impact Squad as well as Federal Bureau of Investigation agents kept up their surveillance, but there was no sign of Stander.

Unmarked trucks patrolled the area and men had concealed themselves in adjacent premises.

At 10.30 pm a young member of the Tactical Impact Unit, Officer Michael von Stetina, was sitting in an unmarked truck with Anthony Tomasello keeping observations.

Tomasello takes up the story.

'We saw a gentleman leaning on a fence with a bicycle. As we turned round to get a better look, he started riding.

'He headed towards us. As he came level with us, I said it was the same guy. He was wearing a black and grey cap.

'We continued on and heard on the radio that he was standing in a car port.

'We turned around and confronted him as he rode towards us again. I said: "That's him, That's him."

'The officer cut off his path.

'He ran into the driveway with his bicycle. Officer von Stetina leapt out yelling "Halt, Police".'

Stander ran off.

'His backpack fell off and I picked it up.

'The neighbours were coming out and I pushed them back inside. Then I heard one shot, then a series of shots.

'The officers then came back and told me they had shot him.'

Other sources enlarge on this story from the moment Officer von Stetina decided to effect Stander's arrest.

They say that Officer von Stetina left his unmarked vehicle and approached the cyclist. He was armed with a shotgun and a holstered handgun – standard issues for the local Florida police.

He crossed the street and approached the suspect.

'Halt, Police!' he shouted to him.

Stander, clearly surprised by the unexpected actions of the police officer, dropped his bicycle and attempted to escape. These were destined to be the last few steps he would ever take.

Stander ran towards the apartment block where he lived and into the driveway with Officer von Stetina in hot pursuit.

It was raining heavily and he slipped and fell in the driveway when von Stetina was only meters away from him

'Okay, I Give Up'

Stander got up, raised his hands in the air and shouted, 'Okay, I give up.'

Still von Stetina rushed at him, his shotgun ready for action and told him to get back on the ground.

When they were within arms length of each other, Stander lunged for the shotgun.

Von Stetina hit Stander with the butt. The stock broke off and in the struggle in the teaming rain a wild shot went off.

Von Stetina's colleagues levelled their guns, thinking

their colleague was in danger.

Stander finally got possession of the damaged but still fireable shotgun and tried to make a run for it. At the end of the driveway, he found himself facing a fence. There was no way he could scale it.

He turned and held the shotgun in a firing position. It was his favoured weapon and the one he knew best.

Simultaneously von Stetina drew his service pistol and opened fire.

'He's Hit'

Stander fell on the driveway, the shotgun clattering from his grip.

He had been fatally wounded.

With only minutes left to live, his hands were unceremoniously pulled behind his back and his wrists manacled.

He lay there and died in the driveway of the apartment block, his blood spreading crimson patterns in the water puddles.

Mark Dane who lives one street away from where the shooting occurred said: 'I heard a shot and a little pause, then rapid fire. Then I heard a shout: '"He's hit."'

Dane added: 'I didn't come outside right away, because you never know who's going to come running through the backyard.'

The Police had got their man.

Stander's Last Grand

When they then searched his flat they found several colour photographs of his prized possession, the transiently owned *Lily Rose,* as well as four thousand six hundred dollars in cash; also three South African Books of Life in the names of Lourens Johannes Mostert, Malcolm Dennis Jennings and Edwardo Christo de Villiers. There were also passports in the names of Brian Kenny and Peter Hillary Harris – stolen from the tellers at the Volkskas Bank at Jan Smuts Airport.

They discovered further proof of Stander's fetish for spectacles, as there were ten pairs there in all, including sunglasses. There was, too, a skipping rope, jogging clothes and a variety of sporting gear.

His luggage contained suede and leather jackets and one or two suits.

A later search of his car revealed nothing but a used prophylactic.

Fall from Grace

A battered Mustang with a used prophylactic inside, a bike and a scruffy flat; how the high living robber had fallen from grace. Yet, although he might have been down, he certainly didn't behave as if he was out. He had joined a local squash racquet club as well as the Beach Port Bunny Club.

A spokesman for the Bunny Club stated: 'We were shocked to hear that he was South Africa's most wanted man because whenever he came here he had charm, style and class.'

Even though he was in arrears with his rent, his landlady, Stella Lanardos, said: 'He was polite and respected me as a landlady. He might have done all that stuff but I can't say anything bad about him. He was nice to me.'

Stander remained an enigma, even after his death. He could still sway people with his charm.

The Americans, with the evidence in their hands, were convinced they had killed the wanted fugitive. But the South Africans needed to be certain. The fingerprint form, sent from Pretoria, had still not reached the Federal Bureau of Investigation. Almost immediately another set was placed on a plane to the United States.

Most of South Africa sat back with mixed feelings and anxiously awaited the verdict.

Was South Africa's most hunted villain and instant hero dead or alive?

Had the Fort Lauderdale police made a mistake?

Inevitable Death

André Stander's father knew from the first mention in the South African press that it was likely his son had been shot dead – that he would never see him alive again.

For forty eight hours after the initial reports of the shooting, South Africa waited. At 8.00 pm (South African time) on Wednesday night, theaf01 Medical Examiner's Office in

Fort Lauderdale made the announcement.

André Charles Stander was dead. There was no doubt about it. The man who robbed with a gun in hand had died by the gun, shot three times.

The rogue ex-policeman who had thought he knew it all had been stopped by another policeman who knew his job better.

The master of disguise hadn't been able to conceal his accent and he blundered around in a strange environment like a grounded whale.

What's more, he had died alone and far from home.

Yet, in spite of all that, he had gone down fighting. This was the stuff of legends. Like Bonnie and Clyde, or Butch Cassidy and Billy the Kid.

The real truth of who and what he was started to ebb away along with André Stander's life blood on that cold and wet concrete driveway.

Doubt, bitterness, acrimony, disbelief, official versions and unofficial versions abounded.

Press razzmatazz swiftly followed the official announcement of his dramatic end.

The myths started to grow, feeding on the aftermath of his death. A new legend sprang up fully grown from the roots of the many unsolved mysteries surrounding him, the missing links and the niggling uncertainties.

Many South Africans wanted to deny the certainty of Stander's death.

10

Unsolved Mysteries

Despite the public clamour, rumours and doubts, the basic facts of the Stander dossier were clear. This is the police report on the Stander gang's activities since Thursday the 11th August 1983. From the time Stander and McCall escaped from prison the gang was sought in connection with:
Escaping – three counts,
Armed robbery – 27 counts,
Attempted murder – one count,
Car theft – six counts,
Rape – one positive count, actually two,
Kidnapping – three counts,
Their total haul including cash, weapons and cars totalled R664 868.

During the course of their investigations, the Police took possession of the following:
Three twelve-bore shotguns,
One .223 mini rifle,
One .357 Magnum revolver,
Four 9mm pistols,
Three .38 Special revolvers,
One thousand four hundred rounds of ammunition; and
Two telescopic sights.

Police issued an inventory of the cash and loot they recovered during the course of the investigations.

Cash – R48 460 (including foreign currency and bank drafts),

Six luxury cars valued at R132 600, One four wheeled drive vehicle valued at R10 500,

One motorcycle valued at R600,

The *Lily Rose* yacht valued at R219 000,

The four wheel drive vehicle, the yacht and the bike had actually been bought by the gang during their spree.

Those are the bald facts.

Slanging Match

After the formal announcement of Stander's death, the slanging match began.

'Why,' asked General Stander, 'did the American police have to shoot a man on a traffic violation? Surely a South African agent was involved.'

But the South African Police have denied the allegation at the highest level. General Christie Zietsman, Chief of the Criminal Investigation Department, said no South African policeman was ever sent to the United States to hunt for Stander. The South Africans cooperated with their American counterparts at the highest level using diplomatic channels to make contact. Details of the flat address in Fort Lauderdale, the Ford Mustang car and the bicycle were all sent to the United States by the South African Police. The legal process for Stander's extraditions, should he be apprehended, were put in motion long before his death.

Warrants for Stander's arrest had been prepared in South Africa and the Americans were informed of the details.

A woman lawyer had been briefed in the USA to handle the details of the extradition.

But the only part of Stander which was extradited were his ashes. He was cremated in Fort Lauderdale six days after his death.

Press Row

Then came the press row, when the Ministry of Law and

Order appeared piqued by the openness of the United States police officials. After the death of Stander, and after the Press had been informed by the American police that the man they had shot dead was believed to be South Africa's most wanted fugitive, a row broke out in South Africa.

The Minister of Law and Order, Mr Louis le Grange, said in a statement:

'I have been informed by the Commissioner of the South African Police, General Johann Coetzee, that André Stander, the fugitive former policeman, has been positively identified by the United States Police as the person who was shot dead in Fort Lauderdale, Florida earlier this week.

'I regret that this former policeman had to die in such a manner, but as he chose a career of crime and violence, I do not wish to comment on his life style.

'I do, however, wish to express my condolences to his parents. His father is a respected, retired, very senior officer of the South African Police.

'I regard it as unfortunate that the United States Police thought it fit to first inform the news media of the positive identification of Stander before informing the South African Police.'

These words caused a storm in the local Press.

The Minister was slammed for his comments on the American way of handling the media. It most certainly does not happen in South Africa. The Minister's statement was clarified by General Zietsman, who criticised the American Police for turning the Fort Lauderdale shooting into a 'publicity stunt'.

'They were more interested in advertising than in supplying us with information.'

General Zietsman also explained: 'In South Africa it is our job to withhold the name of any person dying of unnatural causes until the next-of-kin has been officially informed. We had given Stander's father an undertaking that he would be the first to know about any developments which were made in the investigations into his son's activities.'

But General Stander was to learn of his son's death through the newspaper reports, even though he had not by then been officially identified by comparison of fingerprints.

It had happened to McCall's brother, Peter, as well. He had caught a tail end snippet of a news flash, and had then telephoned the *Rand Daily Mail* and got details of his brother's death in the Houghton shoot out.

. He commented that he was very angry to learn of his brother's death only via the media. The TV shots of the siege had also greatly upset him, he said.

The American police, especially those in Fort Lauderdale, were extremely cooperative when it came to dealing with the Press.

The first reports had reached South Africa at about 10.00 am on the 14th February – Saint Valentine's Day.

Many trans-Atlantic telephone calls from South African journalists were answered cheerfully and helpfully by the Fort Lauderdale police officers even though it was only 3.00 am there.

Unexpected Pleasure

It was an unexpected pleasure for South African newsmen who normally deal with police matters to find such open cooperation, especially at such an early hour.

Information, too, was forwarded without hesitation and interviews with the officers involved were readily given.

Even so, though the entire picture was quickly put into public perspective, the South African Police were officially left in the dark.

Details of the shooting were given to the South African Police by the Johannesburg Press – long before they were told anything by their American counterparts.

But after the Press furore died down, many letters to newspapers supported the more open American approach to crime fighting; for example, as in two letters to the *Star*, published during February 1984:

Thanks USA
   The Minister of Law and Order, Mr le Grange, appears

to know little regarding reporters on Police station duty in the US, especially when rumours had been buzzing round.

On the spot media reporting is part of the everyday life there and one would assume that no 'D' Notice applies to a foreign criminal.

Far better he thanks the American police.

Interested Reader

Springs

Secrecy Disease

Mr Louis le Grange complains the the media were informed before the South African Police of the end of the sordid Stander saga.

We, on the other hand, should be thankful for this. The 'secrecy' disease, rampant in the Defence Force, would no doubt have infected the local police; and we South Africans would, for an unspecified period, have been the only people in the world not to know that Stander was dead.

Colin Melville

Melrose

The Americans have a different way of operating. Perhaps they understand that only the suppressed word is dangerous. Public curiosity feeds on rumour.

Alive or Dead?

The first question after Stander's shooting was: is he really dead? Stander's admirers willed that he should escape.

The ridiculous permutations of fantasy are many: Why was he cremated? Why were the fingerprints lost or delayed? Well, hint the conspiracy mongers, he was given a new identity in America by 'them' . . . whoever they are . . . and now he is free . . . back home after plastic surgery. The body was somebody else's, although the fingerprints matched . . . they had been taken from the live Stander, not the dead replacement.

Stander is definitely alive, we are told, because there

have been numerous sightings of him in South Africa since the 13th February, presumably as accurate as the hundreds of false eye witness accounts before he fled to America.

Stander is dead, no matter how much the hero worshippers want him to be alive. Credulity is the very stuff of myths.

During his crime spree, Stander was thought to be everywhere, like some super speed Scarlet Pimpernel. One minute he was said to be preparing to rob the Rhema Church in Johannesburg – all that money and no guns to protect it . . . and the next he had James Bonded his way into securing a list of tapped telephones . . . then he was supposed to have been seen fishing with senior policemen.

Everybody had discovered – or invented – a Stander story. Everybody claimed to know him or a mutual friend. The hints of police collusion were common. Sure, Stander . . . who had obvious reserves of charm . . . must have had one or two old friends in the South African Police. But there can be no evidence of police connivance in either the escape or continued freedom of ex-Captain Stander – to the contrary, as a matter of pride, let alone duty, the Police were determined to nail him and in the end he was nailed.

Collusion?

A Prison Department enquiry right at the start considered the question of collusion in the escape of Stander. Collusion, it was found, did not exist, but there were grounds for criticism of negligence.

What happened to McCall's photograph?

The escape had been carefully planned for years, obviously with some outside preparation. The yacht plan in particular had taken five years to mature.

It must be remembered, though, that no matter how alert and watchful guards are they cannot give a hundred percent of their attention at all times.

The prisoner with escape on his mind has all the time in the world to plan it. He merely waits for the right moment, which may not come very often, and then he grabs it.

Stander's 'right moment' took over three years to come.

Then came the much publicised encounters with the

Police. It was understandable bad luck that the policemen who encountered Stander during the video shop raid did not recognise him. After all, he was a master of disguise. Again, the men who called from Norwood police station, a mile from Stander's Houghton hideout, must have kicked themselves afterwards when they discovered they had unwittingly called on South Africa's Public Enemy Number One.

Perhaps the South African Police unofficially regret, too, not grabbing Stander in Lesotho, despite the diplomatic problems it might have caused.

According to Mrs Henn, a detective also stood next to the gang in the Randburg gun shop.

Then there was the rumour that the South African Police had sent a man to work with the Fort Lauderdale Police two weeks before Stander's death.

It was even suggested that the reluctance of the local police to allow Officer von Stetina to be photographed suggested that a South African agent had actually nailed his compatriot Stander.

Pure Moonshine

Much of the final conjecture about Stander is based upon pure moonshine.

Certainly Stander dented the reputation of the South African Police but in the end they had still got him.

Police forces can overcome their dents – criminals who make mistakes can't.

It is strange really that overseas South Africa is often called a police state. Yet, compared with European countries, South Africa is proportionately underpoliced.

In America, New York City has roughly the same number of policemen as the total in South Africa (which in recent years has averaged about thirty five thousand regulars). But the South African Police has to contend with a violent society. Soweto, for example, has a homicide rate which is proportionately seven times higher than New York's. Nation wide, the latest figures for murders reported increased from 8 084 (1981/82) to 8 573 (1982/83) but the number of robberies and rapes – the reported ones –

decreased by 397 to 38 229 and 193 to 15 342. But the figures for burglary, car theft and serious assault increased in comparison with the previous years.

Unlike the American police forces, the South African police, besides contending with the world wide police staffing problems, must perform counter insurgency tasks on the border.

Although it might be frequently criticised, the Force is tough and efficient.

One of the strong points of the South African Police is its successful operation of a very extensive informer network. However, with the Stander gang, although some information did filter through about Stander from informers, it wasn't enough for the Police to achieve an early arrest.

Some people took comfort from the misfortunes of the law while others gently mocked their predicament. As a humorous column in the *Finance Week* put it:

Now that fugitive André Stander is no more, life in the Criminal Investigation Department returns to normal. It happens not without a certain despondency.

There are cops who, for weeks, have been determinedly searching for Stander day in and day out at the Wanderers cricket, in the bar at the Oxford Hotel, on Clifton beach, fishing at Langebaan . . .

Rape

It was even mooted that the Police had come up with falsified evidence of the Stander rape case in order to blacken his folk hero image. This, though, is what really happened.

In October 1983 Randburg detectives were called in to search for a young man who had raped a sixteen year old Johannesburg schoolgirl who worked as a part time photographic model. A man later alleged to be Stander telephoned modelling agencies and obtained telephone numbers of the models with offers of photographic assignments.

He arranged to meet the girl at the popular Kyalami Ranch hotel. This hotel, situated north of Johannesburg, is used by the world's top racing drivers when they are competing at the nearby race track.

The beautiful, retiring young girl arrived, after the man

had made arrangements with her mother. The assignment she was going on was completely above board, or so she thought.

After Stander took shots of her fully clothed he suddenly attacked and raped her. Afterwards, the rapist drove the hysterical girl home. Violence and a lift home, again the

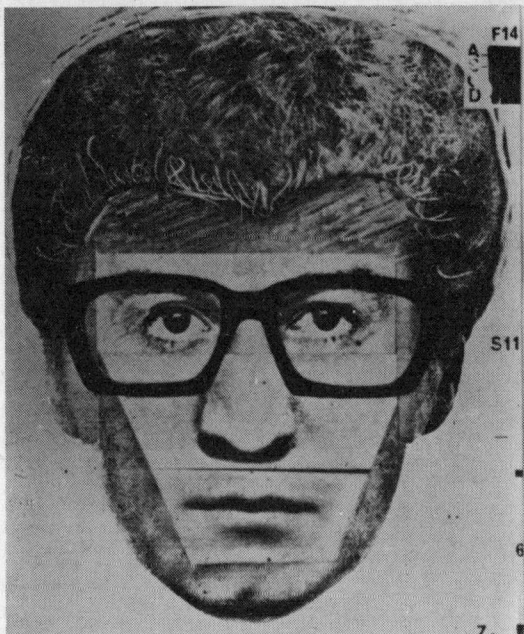

The identikit issued by the police after the rapes were reported.

paradox of crime and convention in Stander's career, or was the more likely explanation that he didn't want her creating a scene at the hotel?

On the way home Stander did not comfort the traumatised girl. Instead, he threatened to 'cut her face to pieces' so that she would never be recognisable, if she informed on his savage deed.

The sensitive young girl is still severely damaged psychologically.

Police File

At the time of the rape in October, the Police issued a description of the rapist which was remarkably similar to Stander's. An identikit picture was broadcast on SABC-TV's *Police File* programme. The rape victim also positively identified Stander from police photographs.

That was the formality.

But, every time Stander's picture was featured in the media, she re-lived her personal agony and burst into tears – because she had no doubt at all as to the identity of her attacker.

Photographs of the rape victim, modelling shots taken in the hotel room by the accused, were found at the scene of the Houghton shootout – which is conclusive evidence that Stander was the culprit.

Stander also raped a another teenage girl using the same *modus operandi*.

The so called 'gentleman robber' had acted out of character, at least so far as his so called romantic image was concerned. A policeman who had served with him in Kokstad, and who knew him very well, said: 'I was shocked to hear he was connected to the rape cases. He had all the women he wanted at his fingertips.'

Louis Kruger, another old comrade and friend from the Force, said: 'Although the dollies loved him, he was no Don Juan.' He, too, was very surprised at the rape accusation.

'He was very popular among women. It was not in his nature to be like that. It must have been in goal that he became like that. He must have gone off the rails.'

No matter how strong the facts of the rape case were, the general public was incredulous.

A letter to the *Sunday Times* aptly summed up the public mood:

I just wish everyone would now leave André Stander in peace: he's paid the supreme penalty for his misdeeds now let us leave him alone.

*Of course, our Police do not help matters by carrying
on about him. Now they accuse him of being a rapist.*

*Next thing I suppose they'll be accusing him of the wave
of pick pocketing in Central Johannesburg.*

Unbelieving, Commissioner Street, Johannesburg

Regarding these criticisms of the Police it must be said
that the South African Police were unlucky not to spot
Stander in their accidental brushes with him. Further, the
evidence of collusion or fabrication of evidence is non exist-
ent and the allegation ridiculous in any case.

It is part and parcel of the Stander mythification.

Some of the published press reports are simply mislead-
ing. Reports that the Police were seeking Peter Hosford,
the would-be skipper of the *Lily Rose,* were false. Before
he set sail for Fort Lauderdale in the *Probust* on the 4th
February, he had been completely cleared by the Cape
Town Police.

He was the man who tipped off the Police that Stander
wanted to buy the *Lily Rose.*

Ian Allen, the broker who received thirteen thousand
rand for selling Bill Cooper's yacht to Stander, left South
Africa to settle in Fort Lauderdale in the middle of February. He sold up his house and decided to settle with his
family in America. Although the departure of the two men
was given sinister overtones in newspaper reports, Allen's
trip had been planned for a long time.

Both men had fully assisted Cape Town police and were
in no way implicated with the gang.

Merely a Traffic Offence

General Stander has also been given a great deal of newspaper space. Although the massive amount of letters of
support and condolence he received indicated some public
sympathy, his actions did not befit a former Police officer of
high rank no matter how acute was his personal agony.

Superficially his complaint about a traffic offence leading
to his son's death is convincing. As he put it: 'The only offence he had committed in America was apparently to have
gone through a red robot. Since when do the American

Police shoot minor traffic offenders?

'If that happened in South Africa, the policemen would immediately have been arrested?'

Officer von Stetina, after a departmental enquiry, was to be the subject of a grand jury hearing. This is routine under American law when someone dies as a result of police action. The grand jury met in camera in a small courtroom in Fort Lauderdale on 7th March. Michael von Stetina presented a statement through his attorneys which said he had fired at Stander because he thought his life was in danger. The verdict reached was justifiable homicide. The matter would go no further.

General Stander also asked: 'They say he was resisting arrest . . . on what charge? As far as I know no warrant had been sent to American for his arrest.'

Well, he was wrong. There was a warrant and the South African Police had gone through the correct channels to ask the American Police to get their man.

General Stander's defence of his son, although understandable, is too simplistic. Maybe he is not the only father guilty of it, but there seems to have been a situation where both during and after his son's police service, he was far too protective.

The Tembisa allegations, made during and after the first trial, are certainly unconvincing.

The General also publicly refused to help the Police.

After his son's death he admitted he knew his son was in America, although he denied having any direct contact with him. He said André had passed on messages by telephoning family and friends at random.

He denied that Heyl had sneaked into America with him saying: 'I knew André was in America, but it's a lot of nonsense that Heyl went with him, although he may also be in America now.'

Play the Game

Immediately after Stander's escape on Thursday the 11th August 1983, senior police officers approached General Stander 'and asked him to play the game'. He agreed.

However, he kept a lot back and this is hardly playing the

146

game.

He allowed his private grief to affect his public duty. The clear duty of any citizen of the country, let alone a former police officer.

Yet, in spite of it all, General Stander's awful dilemma, the dreaded nightmare of any parent, cannot be dismissed that simply. He was certainly more deserving of sympathy than his hoodlum son.

Other major questions remain. Much of the ambiguity of the Stander saga was caused by the gang leader's complex, perhaps even schizoid, personality. Was he a good man who became bad? A brilliant cop and brilliant criminal? Or was he, as some of his former colleagues now say he was, a lousy detective, and, as his final blunders suggest, a pretty useless criminal as well.

McCall

There are a number of key questions about McCall. One of the first was the nature of his accident. The Ford stolen by Stander from Mrs van Staden was crashed on the 10th October. Some evidence – the description of the driver, clothing and the nature of injuries – suggests that McCall could be the driver. But exactly a month later, McCall scrambled over the gun shop counter in Randburg. He had also previously managed to rob banks and spring Heyl . . . hardly the activities of a man crippled with a broken jaw and leg.

Who was the mystery man in that crash? On a number of occasions it seems the gang employed extra recruits. And the driving record of the gang, speeding around the country, could have produced two accidents by three to five men in a six months period in a variety of stolen cars. So, either a fourth or fifth man was in the Ford, or McCall suffered minor injuries?

But McCall was seen by a number of eye witnesses up to late December wearing plaster on one leg and his jaw wired up. Mrs Jenny Peters, the owner of the Linmeyer house, mentioned it, so did Mrs Barkhuizen.

Interestingly, the video shop owner says that McCall had two legs in plaster and he was 'speaking skew with his mouth half-closed'. She says they talked about the dangers of drunken driving, particularly in the festive season. McCall, says Mrs Barkhuizen, indicated that he had been both in a motor accident and in intensive care. But the two legs in plaster seems odd. Was this an elaborate ruse?

Hardly. Why should a fugitive, who needed to be alert, hamper his own movements. Both contacts of McCall and the Police confirm that he was out of action for at least six weeks. Police say that Heyl and Stander acted alone during a crucial stage of the bank hopping spree.

Mrs Barkhuizen, who initially confused the identification of Stander and McCall, admitted to being unsure of the exact time when she saw McCall's injuries. It seems likely that McCall crashed shortly after the gun shop raid, and did suffer serious injuries. But the exact nature and timing of those injuries can only be confirmed by access to hospital records, and even this will be of little use unless the false name he used while a patient there can be confirmed.

But how exactly did McCall die? Did he commit suicide just before the final shootout? Or was he killed by police bullets?

Was McCall shopped by Stander, who in one vague version of a story is also said to have killed Heyl?

His brother, Peter McCall, a professional man in Johannesburg, initially said: 'The potential of them having shopped him is high.

'I would like to believe he wasn't and I'm going to believe he wasn't because that is what I want to believe. Any kind of vindictive feelings dissolved when André died.'

Betrayal?

There were arguments for and against Stander setting up McCall. Certainly Stander wrote the Houghton shootout address at the Cape Sun Hotel when he registered there during negotiations to buy the yacht. He was staying there himself then, but he presumably knew McCall would be there after he left for America.

Peter McCall said: 'The Cape Sun address might have been Stander setting him up. But it was very risky though.' McCall, because he was incapacitated with a broken leg, did not take part in all the robberies. Was there an argument about a three way split in the loot?

Two weeks before the shootout they pooled all the money – presumably to pay for the yacht.

Did McCall want out with his share of the money?

The girls from the escort agencies who comforted the gang on the run noticed signs of tension and disagreement. McCall was certainly an independent sort of person; he might not have always accepted the decisions of the domineering Stander.

But other arguments run counter to the betrayal theory. McCall was due to sail on the yacht, an important part of the escape plan. And, as Peter McCall explained, his brother always carried a little note book in which he jotted things. 'Stander must have been aware that he had a note book if he had been in any kind of intimate contact with Leigh for six months. He must have been aware that he writes things down and keeps things.

'I find it very difficult to believe that Stander would have done that (betray Leigh) because Stander would have run great risks.

'Maybe Stander was the fool. My brother wrote things down and maybe he was supposed to commit this American address to memory. Maybe that was his guarantee: if I go, you go too.'

Another factor was loyalty. Stander seemed to be a very loyal friend. He had sprung Heyl, and covered for McCall when he had his car accident. Stander had been done unto, as far as he was concerned, by Cor van Deventer. Was Stander really likely to risk his own neck by shopping McCall? Besides, Stander spent time at the Houghton shootout address too.

McCall's death poses other questions for his family. Peter McCall regarded the use of forty plus crack policemen armed with grenades and rifles as rather excessive for one man.

'If the Police had the house under surveillance for all that time, they must have known that there was only one person in that house,' he maintained.

'The view has been expressed that there were three cars, so therefore the Police thought there were three of them. You can't buy that.'

Police Brutality?

So if they perhaps knew that only one man was there, why such a display of force, asked the brother. 'The family are very upset about the level of police brutality in the final analysis.'

But the unarguable facts were that McCall was armed, dangerous and desperate. He had shot one woman during the course of an armed robbery and wounded a policeman during the shootout.

It was clear that on the balance of probabilities he could well have to face the death penalty if he were arrested and tried for his crimes.

Policemen have a duty to perform, and they often have to face risks unappreciated by the public.

Take one year as an example. In 1981 ten policemen were killed and sixty six seriously injured in the execution of their duties, excluding those killed or injured in motor vehicle accidents.

Clearly there are two sides to every gun.

Peter McCall also asked why only five thousand rand was found at the shoot out scene? Had, in fact, a lot more been found, speculated McCall, or had Stander really left Patrick Leigh McCall in the lurch with just a tiny fraction of the loot?

Heyl

In the end the McCall mysteries may be answered only if and when Heyl and the other real mystery man or men are caught. But will they, particularly Heyl, escape the net?

For the sake of the legend, many must hope that Heyl remains at large. He was considered to be the weak link but he has survived.

Fate proved the other two weaker for they were shot dead.

Part of the image of his weakness was created by the false assumption that Heyl was merely the driver in most of the bank hopper raids. In fact, for two months while McCall was out of action with a broken leg and jaw, Heyl played a central role in the bank robberies.

Maybe it's a question of professions; maybe it's psychologically easier to believe that a tough cop or parabat can become a tough robber, but Heyl always retained the image of a mild mannered school teacher. The use during his early days of crime of a toy gun, too, enhanced the characterization of his being 'soft'.

But he was a convicted bank robber.

Heyl is on the run, but where? A good bet is the United Kingdom, but some clues link him to the United States. American police and the Federal Bureau of Investigation were investigating the possibility that Heyl met Stander the day before he was killed.

The Colt Python .38 pistol bought by Stander is missing. Does Heyl have it?

Where did Stander go on that long car journey at Fort Lauderdale just before he died? When he borrowed a car from Anthony Tomasello he said: 'I've got a very important meeting at Shooters at 6.00 pm and I can't miss it.' Yet, when the car was returned to Tomasello the next morning it was full of sand and had used a full tank of petrol, enough to travel at least two hundred and fifty kilometers.

Heyl in America?

Tomasello later claimed the reward of at least R85 000 which he believed (wrongly) had been offered by the South African Police and Clearing Bankers' Association and which he had earned by his tip off which led to Stander's death.

It was a tip off he soon began to regret. Tomasello told police he had received two telephone calls allegedly from Heyl whom he was convinced was in America.

The garage owner said: 'The first time he said, "I'm coming to get you." I thought, "Nah, it's a prank."

'Twenty minutes later he called again. This time he said: "I'm a dead man anyway, so I'm out to avenge my partner."'

Frightened, Tomasello moved his pregnant wife and two children out of town. Was it a crank, or was it really Heyl?

The South African Police are not sure. But General Zietsman added: 'We are not giving up. The Police have made some deductions because not all the photographs in the identity books found in André Stander's apartment were of him.'

Central Question

Tomasello poses one of the central questions of the mystery. If the South African Police had done so much to aid the American police, why was Tomasello's tip off so vital?

If the Fort Lauderdale Police had the addresses of Stander, then surely he would have been under constant surveillance from the time they realised he was not just a traffic offender.

If the American police had such important information on Stander, why did Tomasello have to lead the Police to him – after a mere accidental perusal of a newspaper.

The South African Police claimed that they gave specific information about Stander's racing bicycle, the Mustang and his addresses to the American police. But how could they know about such details if they didn't have men on the spot? It is possible that an informer who was after the reward telephoned Pretoria directly, but he would more likely have gone directly to his own police force. Maybe he contacted both?

The Extra Men

Heyl, the third identified man, has escaped . . . for the time being. The two men who helped in the Randburg gun shop raid have been unidentified. Perhaps they were small time criminals or personal friends of the gang. Earlier Stander had agonies about trusting people. But later his carefree security had allowed him to leave accurate addresses in hotels and shops and to trust a wide range of girlfriends, paid and volunteer. Getting in a few 'gofers' – men who would run around for the trio – does not seem implausible.

After McCall's injuries, extra help was especially useful. Stander did hit banks on his own without a driver in his first robbery spree in the 1970s. And the police have confirmed that some raids were done by Heyl and Stander alone. Leaving a car engine running while you rob banks is risky.

A getaway driver is standard crooked practice. When McCall was laid up, a so far unidentified crook may have stood in for him as a driver.

But the substitute driver or the extra hands in Randburg were small fry. Was there a more important fourth man with the same standing in the gang as Stander?

Initially both the South African Police and the FBI thought they had found him. He was a forger who had a long record in America. He arrived in South Africa at the same time as Stander broke out of gaol. By coincidence, he had rented a flat on the same street as Stander's second apartment in Fort Lauderdale. Other links were found. But this was a false trail, no matter how fascinating. The young American was not the fourth man. He could not lead the Police to Heyl or the missing loot.

The Stander operations might have gone beyond just escaping to America with the *Lily Rose*. What was he going to do after that? Stander, remember, was no ordinary criminal. The fact that he had operated so long in his home environment and was fond of family and his ex-wife suggests that he had intended to return at some time to South Africa. He was found with little money and no plans in Fort Lauderdale.

It has been conjectured that Stander grabbed more money than has been publicised. This money or at least the money from the bank robberies so far accounted for, plus the sale of the yacht, no doubt after a lengthy tropical cruise, could then have been laundered into a legal business in South Africa. A fourth man, probably an outsider and a South African, would likely have set up a company to legally invest the gang's ill-gotten assets. Here again Heyl could be the key to the mystery.

11

In Memoriam

Stander was cremated in America, and the ashes took their time returning home.

General Zietsman said that he hoped 'the ghost of André Stander will now be laid to rest'.

It was not to be: the immediate public reaction to his death was dramatic. A book, films and a song were instantly promised.

(The song – *Didn't We Hope It Wasn't Your Feet,* - was not written to glorify Stander. 'We are not trying to commercialise his death or to make a hero of him,' said the composer.

Mr Torr, an economics lecturer in Pietermaritzburg, composed it and Miss Laurika Rauch added the melody. The song was intended to comment on the public reaction to the saga . . . 'more about us than him,' said Mr Torr. The song's title refers to the brief glimpse TV viewers had of the dead man's feet as Stander was loaded into the ambulance. The song tries to capture the mood of the public which 'hoped it wasn't him' . . . before the final identification was confirmed.

Sentimentality oozed from the public.

One grandmother said: 'He captured all our imagination.

I used to read every word printed about him. We were all rooting for him. He had style.

Another Stander observer said: 'I know there must be justice, but somehow he just deserved to get away. He never hurt anyone really.'

Obviously his friends mourned him. One of his girl friends, Sue Hewitt, who knew him as Mark, said on hearing the news: 'Oh my God, not Mark . . . I only ever saw the good side of Mark. I had no idea who he was until the newspaper carried the report of his friend's death.'

A woman friend who didn't want to be identified said: 'In my eyes André did these things because his life was boring. To him, it was like a game of cops and robbers and he was intelligent enough to know he was going to be caught.'

Louis Kruger, his old pal from Kempton Park police station, was so cut up that he went on a drinking spree for three days.

Some expressed outrage at the manner of Stander's death.

In the *Star* 'Disgusted' of Kensington said:

'I think people today are more barbarous than ever. I refer to the shooting of André Stander. Surely there are different ways to catch a thief? And let me tell the American Police they are cowards. You don't even shoot a dog.

My deepest sympathy with his family.

Not everyone was so sentimental.

Die Volksblad said:

'André Stander died as he would not wish to have done: as a pathetic man on a bicycle . . . after a string of luxury motor cars.'

What did other policemen feel, those who were not his personal friends? A captain in one of the crack Murder and Robbery Squads, the same age as Stander, said: 'I would have liked seeing Stander before the court. Then I believe all the grandeur of the man would have paled into insignificance once you prove what kind of man he was.'

What did Stander's ex-best friend, Cor van Deventer, feel? His initial reply when asked about Stander's death was: 'Well, first of all it's good for the banks and the build ing societies.'

Stander's immediate family grieved, but only his father publicly lashed out at the manner of his son's killing.

Then, on Sunday the 4th March 1984, came the memorial service at the Hartebeespruit Nederduitse Gereformeerde Church, Harris Street, Pretoria. Amid the red and white carnations quiet dignity prevailed. It was a time for the family to weep.

Thousands were expected, but two hundred friends and family and a small gaggle of pressmen paid their final respects.

The preacher, Dominee Grobler, talked about the mysteries and mercy of God. We should not judge others, he said, 'but we must look at our own lives.'

The short simple service was led with a text from Romans, Chapter 14, verse 9: 'For Christ died and rose to life in order to be the Lord of the living and dead.'

General Frans Stander, wearing dark glasses, barely suppressed his grief during the service. He was shielded by family. Bekkie, André's twice married former wife, shared the family's tragedy.

After the service, a friend, Frik Kruger, thanked the public for the many cards, letters and flowers from people of all races.

Two well dressed black women, who said they had worked for André Stander, said their farewells too.

Stander was dead, but the myth still lived on.

12

The Other Woman

Stander was often portrayed as a beast. But to the woman who claims to have known him best of all, he was the most tender and loving of men. Hèléne (her surname was withheld by the authors) was first mistress and then close confidante of the crook for over ten years.

Stander left his wife, Bekkie, for Hèléne and proposed to her.

For two years after they met in 1969 they were lovers. Then, over the years, their passionate relationship became more a close friendship and intellectual companionship.

In her first ever interview, Hèléne was determined to put the picture right about her ex-lover. Her account sheds fascinating new light on Stander's personality, but she was also deeply in love with the man. She would brook no criticism of him. She point blank refused to believe the rape allegation even when she was presented with the facts by the authors.

Hèléne – she changed her name – is a sensitive, highly intelligent, artistic woman. She is thirty three, petite, with a delicate elegance and a sharp sense of humour. She is a far cry from the seedy world of call girls and cheap videos. She was a student of classical music and opera.

Hèléne was educated in a strict Catholic convent and is still a practising Roman Catholic. After school, she concentrated on her musical studies in Johannesburg. 'My background was typically European,' she said. Her family came from French and German stock, and music was in their blood.

Drug Raid

She met Stander when her communal student flat was raided for drugs. Stander confiscated some of her political books. They included works by the philosopher Herbert Marcuse.

Stander later read them himself.

She and her flatmate went to see Stander in his Pretoria office. They went out of a mixture of indignation and mischief. 'We wanted to embarrass him because he raided our flat.' Stander was friendly. They asked him to take them back to Johannesburg, and he agreed.

Hèléne and Stander began dating in late 1969. 'In the beginning,' said Hèléne, 'he was very staid, innocent and gullible . . . a typical straight-laced Afrikaans boy. He was very quietly spoken, but he had an ugly high sort of voice which could go almost falsetto.

Right Little Bugger

'He told me he was a right little bugger at school. He told me that he stole his dad's car.'

Stander was eager to join the student set. 'He would have loved to have been a hippy . . . He was intrigued by our life style, the chaos, loud music and that everybody was very happy. It was such a contrast to his staid upbringing. He really envied our freedom,' Hèléne said.

They went to a lot of movies together. They both liked horror shows. One night after watching *Straight Jacket,* starring Joan Crawford, they went back to Hèléne's flat. She was nervous after seeing so much carnage on the screen, with so many bodies being cut up.

Stander went into the flat first and said: 'Don't worry. There's only bits of meat all over the floor. Stander had a very lively sense of humour, of both the sick and subtle variety,' said his former lover.

'He used to read a lot of Ed McBain novels. He loved

Bob Dylan, but didn't like opera or classical music.

Tuned into Police Channels

'He was mad about Bill Cosby. We used to drive around and tune into the CBS (citizen band radio) and the police channels . . . in his own private car.

'André loved socialising. He always dragged me to parties. I prefer to be alone with one person. He used to drink a lot, especially after the Caprivi business (his border duty). He didn't smoke really.'

Hèléne didn't like Stander at first, because he was a policeman. But they soon fell deeply in love. 'We did the silly romantic things . . . walk in the park, climb mountains together.

She even went on police raids with her cop lover.

Stander got to know Hèléne's family well.

They encouraged him to come to the house as often as possible. 'He had a beautiful relationship with my parents. He used to have dinner with them even if I wasn't there.

'He got to know my elder sisters.' One of them, Heather, was a very pretty girl who suffered from toxemia and became very fat. She was very self-conscious about it, but Stander went out of his way to comfort, tease and compliment her to make her feel better. He was exceptionally kind to her over many years, even writing her letters from prison. 'He used to jog past her house every morning and say hello to Heather and try to cheer her up.

Always Lending Money

'He was always trying to help people. Always lending money to people who had fallen on hard times. I used to ask him where he got his money. He said his dad gave it to him, and his brother, Brian, left it to him in a will. That explained it as far as I was concerned.

'He offered to send me to the USA because I was interested in American Indians. "I'll see to it that you go", he said.

'He was very interested in America. I talked to him a great deal about Red Indians. I used to read to him a lot and he listened to me very patiently.'

Stander looked up to the well read, artistic Hèléne. He learned from her. He was always keen to experiment with new experiences. 'We talked about everything, particularly philosophy, but never religion or politics. But we did talk about Indian religion.'

According to Hèléne, Stander was not then a womaniser. He was faithful to his mistress. 'I was never possessive of André and he liked that. He felt free.'

Sexually, said Hèléne, he was a 'very normal man. Very masculine.' Their relationship was sometimes impish. 'He used to walk in as I was getting dressed. He would say, "Come as you are." One day I just had a long blouse on and knickers. He said I must go out like that. And I did.'

They went to a restaurant in Braamfontein.

'I was only twenty then,' she said coyly. 'I would never do it now.

'André had an incredible sense of humour once he was relaxed . . . He was so outrageous. He'd say terrible things about me in company and then wink at me. He was a very naughty boy.

'He always mixed with the wildest people. He really liked a guy who had been married seven times.'

Hèléne said 'I don't know where this business of him being tall comes from. He was compact with very strange hair . . . tight, tight curls . . . like Ethiopian hair . . . light brown. He had hazel eyes with green flecks.'

Got Photographs Back

She said that she took many photographs of André Stander, but he asked for them back plus the negatives and never returned them.

She described his personality. 'He was very, very kind and loyal. He was completely honest. He never lost his temper . . . I never saw him get violent, although he was very tough.

'I was never afraid of him. I always felt very safe with him.

'He wasn't a person to let his emotions show . . . If he got angry his face went red, then immediately afterwards it would go dead pan . . . I have seen André terrified and in total fear . . . or so angry. Then he was so cool and level headed, but it was just an appearance. He used to put on a mask. He was a Scorpio.

'He had a very magnetic personality.'

According to Hèléne, Stander was very punctual and a 'bit of a perfectionist'. Perhaps this was his attempt to match his father.

'He was living his life for his parents at the cost of the loss of his own freedom.

'How come they didn't try to encourage the second son, Brian, to be more than a engine driver? . . . They put a lot of pressure on André; the younger brother didn't have to put up with it at all. 'Nor, presumably, did André's sister.

'He said he admired his father, but he never mentioned that his dad was a general. I found out later from a friend of his.'

André Stander worshipped his younger brother, Brian. 'Brian was a good rugby player. André loved rugby and tug o' war. We used to go often to Ellis Park and Loftus. He was a big supporter of the Springboks.'

Loved Dogs More Than Rugby

Stander loved his dogs even more then rugby. He had eight. 'Five were German shepherds and three were monsters . . . Arnie was the worst. Shalom was a very well trained police dog. He adored Shalom.'

Stander also enjoyed travelling. He used to go for holidays to the South Coast with just his dogs and spend the days roaming with them on the beach. 'He got a taste of high living in Mauritius. He came back with weird ideas about worshipping the sun.'

'Sometimes, Hèléne went with him on his trips.

They used to talk for hours about philosophy. '"What is life about."' he would ask. '"What happens when you end up in the grave? You get eaten by maggots," he would say. 'It's true but that's the fate of us all.'

They talked about life, love and marriage. Like Stander, Hèléne remarried and redivorced the same person. 'André and I kept missing each other. When he was free he was looking for me and when I was divorced I was looking for him.'

Why did Hèléne think that Stander became a crook?

Firstly, she blamed his wife . . . as would most mis

tresses. Then she said that the military action he saw in the Caprivi in 1974 influenced him. 'He got political after that.' Then his counter-insurgency course in 1975; that, too, had an impact on his attitude towards society and the Police, she believed.

But why didn't he just quit the Police?

Hèléne said that his family and friends and even she had encouraged him to stick with it.

Then came Tembisa. 'He told me that he killed a lot of people. He said they shot at chickens, cats, dogs . . . anything that moved.'

According to Hèléne, Stander developed a new attitude towards blacks. 'I've got more respect for my black constables and sergeants than my white superior officers,' he said.

Hèléne knew nothing about Stander's robbery spree in the late 1970s, and she was horrified when she learnt of his arrest.

Husband Ripped Up Letters

Stander wrote letters to her from prison, but her husband used to rip them up. 'He wrote to me about his studies in psychology and philosophy for his BA through UNISA.

Stander wrote to Hèléne's sister. One letter from Zonderwater Prison – with the prison authority's word count on it (letters and wordage are limited according to prisoners' privileges) – it was dated March 1983.

In the letter Stander talks about Hèléne: 'The eternal woman. Her craziness added to her attraction . . . I've always loved her.' Amazingly the letter also says: 'There is so much crime and violence on the East Rand.' Stander worried about Hèléne's sister being alone on the plot when her husband was away. 'Hope Arnie (Stander's dog) gives some protection.'

Hèléne says that Stander was badly treated in prison and his teeth went brown.

So he tried to escape from Pretoria Central. According to Hèléne, he actually got outside with the help of a woman. He was punished with solitary confinement.

She knew nothing of his plans to escape in 1983.

Did he ever try to contact her while he was on the run?

Hèléne explained that she was nearly always at the hospital with her sick baby. Also, she was worried her telephone and the one of her sister, Heather, might have been tapped.

Her sister had a feeling that André used to drive past her house to see Arnie, his demon dog, which she had adopted.

Hèléne would sometimes drive around the Kempton Park area after his escape in the hope of seeing him, but she never laid eyes on him again in her life.

Lift Floorboards

'If André had come to me, I would have given him my car. My mum was prepared to lift the floorboards and hide him . . . We were always hoping that he was going to get away with it and have a good time wherever he went.'

Did she believe he robbed banks?

'Yes, I believe he was a robber. But not a rapist or a killer.'

And the Randburg gun shop?

'He didn't do the shooting.'

But if he was such a caring person why didn't he at least give some first aid to Mrs Henn?

'What did you expect him to do . . . take her to hospital? If he had wanted to kill her, he would have. He was a very good shot.'

America Like A Video

Why did he pick America?

'When I first met him, he wanted to be a narcotics cop in New York. This was his ultimate . . . you know, he'd seen too many videos and films. To him, America was like a video.

'I thought he would go to Brazil. But André loved to be surrounded by familiar places . . . his family and friends. The closest to South Africa was the United States. Europe was too foreign, and in Brazil there was the communication problem. In America he knew the language and the climate and conditions were familiar.

'But he started crumbling in America. He lost his self confidence. He always needed people. He needed approval. He must have got that from Heyl and McCall.'

Then, in a sudden aside, Hèléne shot out: 'Why didn't he rape that stripper if he was such a rapist?'

Hèléne had a premonition about his death: 'I had this incredible dream . . . I was in this flat overlooking the sea. I could see a speedboat with André in it, and another man and woman. I shouted out to André: "I love you. Look after yourself." Then I couldn't see the sea anymore.

'Then he came in and put his arms around my head. He always used to do that . . . it annoyed me. He called me *Kleinkie* and squeezed my head.

'André said: "I've come to say goodbye and to say I love you."

'I told my mum the next day that André was fine and he looked happy. I had that dream two days before he died.

'The terrible part about his death was those two days waiting for the confirmation . . . I was completely devastated. I lost contact with reality. I lived in the past . . . and what I knew of André.

'He was so alone. No one was there to comfort him.'

Love Child

Hèléne then unlocked an unknown secret. André Stander had an illegitimate child. 'He would be about five now. He had supported the child. The baby was the fruit of a casual relationship, but André had met his responsibilities,' said Hèléne.

Did Hèléne think he was a Robin Hood character?

'He was very generous, but no one came forward and said that he was a Robin Hood. No one came up with the proof. And yet, the South African public must be bored if they want to make him a hero.

'Women in this country like macho gangsters and they all fell in love with him. I wonder whether they would have fallen in love with him in 1970?

'He once came down to see me in Durban and asked me to marry him, because I was sick and tired of being a mistress. I was tired of being used.

'I said no, because I thought we would destroy each other. I have something of a death wish too. Perhaps I was wrong, perhaps I could have saved him.'

13

The Leader

André Charles Stander
Age: Thirty seven (born 22/11/1946; died 13/02/1984)
Height: one meter eighty two
Weight: eighty kilograms
Description: A master of disguise, but tall and well built.
Fetish for glasses
Education: Matric
Marital Status: Twice married and twice divorced to Leonie (Bekkie) Stander
Criminal Record
In January 1980, André Stander, formerly Captain Stander of the South African Police, faced twenty eight charges including fifteen counts of armed robbery, attempting to kill a policeman, three counts of possessing firearms, one of forgery, one of uttering, two of stealing firearms, one of fraud and one of conspiracy to escape. He originally pleaded not guilty to all counts, but later changed his plea to guilty on fifteen of them. He was sentenced to seventeen and a half years imprisonment in May 1980.

He escaped on 11th August 1983, sprung fellow prisoner Allan Heyl, led a spree of raids on banks and building societies, an accomplice in the attempted murder by shooting of a Randburg gun shop owner, and finally shot dead by Florida Police on 13th February 1984.

André Stander's father, Frans, was a general in the South African Police. His mother, Violet, was said to be socially conscious, and keen to help her husband's career.

Other members of his well to do and proud family included Dr Ben Stander of Vryheid, who was a doctor of psychology at the University of Pretoria, and Dr Gideon Stander who heads a faculty at the University of Stellenbosch.

Of the Stander family, too, it can never be doubted that there was a good family loyalty, that blood was thicker than water.

His uncle, Mr Nic Stander, said after his death: 'If André had come to me for help he would have been safe in Italy and not in a mortuary. I have an Italian wife and lots of in-laws in Italy. If André had asked I would certainly have helped him to get to Italy and start a new life. If the Police want to lock me up for saying this, I don't care.'

André attended a number of schools as his father rose through the rungs of the Force. André failed matriculation, partly because of his reluctance to study, despite having a good brain. He then matriculated at Police College and became best student of his year in 1964. His first posting was at Rustenburg when André joined the Drugs Squad, his father said that he did not smoke or drink. He was under the command of his father but clashed with his successor who was not, it seems, impressed with his police abilities. He was transferred to Kokstad where he later passed his officers' examination.

André Stander's dissatisfaction with the police, according to his family, reached a peak during the 1976 riots. André Stander was said to have been responsible for the death of twenty two blacks at Tembisa, but this is of doubtful substance.

Loved Blacks

'André loved blacks and always got on very well with his black colleagues, but as a policeman he was forced to shoot kaffirs,' General Stander said.

166

His family maintained that the death of his brother, Brian, in 1978 and the divorce from his wife, Leonie, also deeply affected André. General Stander believes that the drastic personality change which turned a policeman into a dangerous robber was brought about mainly by his experiences in the Police.

André Stander's uncle, Nic Stander, said: 'He had an adventurous spirit which was not used to its full extent in the South African Police . . . His nature was to help people, while he was expected to prosecute as a policeman.'

A fellow gaol mate at Zonderwater, Ferdi van den Bergh, said: 'He believed he was too intelligent to be a policeman . . . He was bored by police work and found it monotonous . . . What he did was for the fun of it, he was no criminal.'

'André was a fine man,' his father said. 'He was well read and educated. I remember how he, as a young boy, used to read hundreds of detective stories.

'He also had a taste for the best things in life. When he went to gaol, he gave me about forty bottles of vintage red wine which he had collected.'

Stander resented the low police pay. He could not afford the luxuries he wanted. His father said it was he who had given Stander the money to renovate his home and buy a swimming pool. He did not lead a high life while he was in the Force, says his father. He loaned the money he got from the robberies to others.

Always Bent

Whether André Stander was always bent is a moot point, but certainly events in his life could have provoked his basic character disorders. He seemed to have had an ambivalent attitude to women. He was said by friends to resent his mother's emphasis on social climbing. His marriage was not successful, but he maintained an excellent relationship with his ex-wife, Bekkie. He was very popular with women, yet he was to become a rapist.

He loved animals, but he severely mistreated his dogs on at least one occasion. He was said to be a gentleman, yet he could threaten to slash the face of a sixteen year old girl. He was charming to his robbery victims, but his steely edge prevented any heroics in the raids. He was reluctant to shoot, but he carried a loaded gun, shot at a policeman and was associated with the shooting of a woman. He loved the high life, but he seemed to be obsessed with a death wish. He was said to be brilliant, yet he failed matric the first time. He didn't read school books, but he loved poetry.

A man who believed in loyalty, and yet is suspected of shopping his partner, McCall. He swore revenge against Cor van Deventer, but did nothing.

'Look, Stander knew me as well as I know him,' said his ex-friend. 'So there was never any chance that he could come around and get me. He knew that I wasn't one of the old ladies, unarmed behind a counter. He knew that I carry a gun, and naturally he would meet with some resistance. I'm glad he didn't come.'

General Stander shared the bitterness of his son, towards Cor van Deventer: 'He knew all along what André was doing but he chose to keep quiet about it until André one day confronted him about irregularities in the business. Then he suddenly ran to the Police.'

General Stander said that he was shocked by a police statement that his son had raped a sixteen year old girl. 'He would never have hurt anybody. He was not the kind of person to cause physical harm to people. It is easy to discredit somebody when he is dead.'

Stander is gone, but the man who would not cause physical harm has left a grievous legacy of psychological hurt to his family and friends. Again, the contradictions – even after his death.

A Man of Refinement

His father said he was a man of refinement, yet he lived a life of booze, low brow videos and call girls when he was on the run. He was a leader, but he copied ideas from McCall or stole them from videos he had watched. One of the videos the gang hired was *Gone in Sixty Seconds* which tells the story of a gang which sets out to steal in one week forty of the world's most exclusive cars. In one sequence, the dare devil gang leader persuades the salesman to change seats during a test drive, then makes off with the car. That is exactly what Stander did to get the Porsche and so did McCall on a number of occasions in his crime career.

The choice of that video also demonstrates Stander's fascination with speed. He drove fast, and got caught going through a robot in Fort Lauderdale when he was supposed to be lying low. Stander was a gutsy, innovative crook, yet he made some of the most elementary errors in the criminal rule book.

An admitted crook who became a friend of Stander, said that the ex-policeman was 'like all romantics, he was an extremist'. The ex-convict who described himself as an 'intellectual crook' – the reason, he said, that Stander befriended him. 'Stander,' he said 'wasn't all Disneyland. Sometimes he was very vicious.'

The criminal got to know Stander's way of thinking.

Why did Stander switch sides?

'He did it because that avenue gave him that great answer to "what is" . . . If it's not enforcing the law, then it's perhaps the opposite. It wasn't for the money even if he might have told himself that.'

Was it the Tembisa business?

'He wasn't a bleeding heart liberal. He wasn't shy of doing what he had to do.'

The former friend of Stander's argued that it wasn't any particular incident that pushed him into crime. It was Stander's own questing personality.

'His whole life was mapped out. He would become a brigadier or general like his father. That's it. He wanted something different. He wanted another life. He was a total romantic. He actually said to me that he wanted to become a writer. But he didn't want to be his dad.'

Why did he act so strangely after coming out of gaol, leaving himself open to recapture?

'Coming out of gaol is like coming out of war . . . there's a great desire to do the opposite: settle down and have a normal life. That's why there's a baby boom after big wars.

'After lying so much in prison, telling the truth is a luxury. Like eating caviar. That's why he put the correct addresses.

'But stealing a car is suicidal. Why steal it? Hire one. You don't steal a car if you're hot. You do everything legit, particularly if you've got money.'

Why did the elusive Stander crumble so quickly in the United States?

Battle Fatigue

'It was battle fatigue. He died of battle fatigue. Nothing to do with actual shooting, but like being in a continual fire-fight. If the birds stop singing, you think it's an ambush. If a little old lady looks at you, you think she's a spy.

'Stealing the car back, admitting to the car salesman who he was, staying in Fort Lauderdale. It was a kind of mechanism of self destruction.

'He didn't have the survival instincts of a crook . . . Because he wasn't forced into it. He'd overcome the primeval dirty hunger to survive. He'd taken his own fate into his hands. That's why he was respected by ordinary criminals.'

In the final analysis Stander was no ordinary crook. He created a legend, like the Foster gang. Maybe he achieved what he set out to achieve.

One friend said of him: 'Being a poet, he was subject to fits of deep depression and moods in which he could see no future and no hope.'

A female friend added: 'In my eyes, André did these things because his life was boring. To him, it was like a game of cops and robbers and he was intelligent enough to know that he was going to get caught.

'He was a Scorpio and he was his own biggest enemy. He turned the sting upon himself.'

Retired Policeman Jack le Grange said of the fugitive on the run: 'Stander has no fear of death. He doesn't mind if they shoot him dead.'

And so despite the Pandora's box of disguises, the chameleonlike existence of André Stander was stopped in a hail of bullets.

A man died and so a myth was born.

14

Man They Shot First

Patrick Leigh McCall
Aged: Thirty four years
Height: One meter seventy five
Description: Slender build, thinning blond hair
Education: Lyttleton Manor High School, Pretoria
Status: Divorced with one child
Criminal Record
- Dates back to 1969 when at the age of twenty he was sent to gaol for three years for car theft. Served eighteen months of sentence.
- In 1975 he stole a car and was fined R80 (or eighty days).
- In January 1976 he was convicted in the Pretoria Regional Court on twenty six charges of theft, fraud, car theft and sentenced to between five and eight years imprisonment.
- In May 1979 he again appeared in court on a charge of car theft and received a further six months.
- In 1980 he escaped from gaol and was on the run for sixteen days. He received a further nine months for escaping.
- He again escaped and was on the run for one hundred and thirty nine days. He also escaped from police custody while awaiting charges of escaping. He was later recaptured and given a further two years for each of the two escapes. In addit-

ion, he was charged with further counts of thefts and car theft, and was declared an habitual criminal and given the indeterminate sentence.

● In August 1983 he escaped with André Stander from a Cullinan physiotherapist. While on the run he robbed banks and building societies as part of the Stander gang, shot and wounded a Randburg gun shop owner and finally died in the Houghton siege in January 1984.

Although the newspapers dubbed Patrick Leigh McCall the 'mystery man' he was well known in his home town of Irene, just outside Pretoria. He attended Lyttleton Manor High School. His father died when he was young, and his mother remarried. His stepfather was described as being 'very kind to Leigh'. He had three brothers and two step brothers.

He was not a tough at school, but 'he could hold his own,' according to schoolfriends. Although he was a good boy scout, he was also very mischievous, always playing pranks like ringing church bells at night. As the best friend of McCall's youth said: 'But then he always did the one little thing too far.'

McCall dropped out of school and studied at a cram college in Pretoria.

He did his military service in the Parabats, but injured his shoulder half way through his service while jumping. He was discharged from national service as a result and he was left with a slight stoop on his left shoulder.

Free Spares

As a teenager he would borrow cars without permission, mainly Minis, go on joyrides and then return them. Later he would just dump them. Then he started keeping them and swopping the engines around.

'He was a real motor enthusiast,' said a friend.

He was popular and likeable. 'He had a way with people,' said his best boyhood friend. 'I never met a guy who could have you rubbing down his car while he would be drinking a beer watching you. He had four of us rubbing down his car once. He was very, very charming.

Eventually, McCall was gaoled for car theft. During his

eighteen months in gaol, he got married to Elizabeth. When he came out of gaol, his friends threw a big party and he went back to his old job which was involved with motor spares. He was described as 'a fantastic worker'.

After a brief period in South West Africa, he went with his wife to Cape Town. Soon a baby boy, Bojo Zacharias, was born. His old friend recalled: 'He used to rock up at my land-lady's on a Saturday morning with the baby to give his wife a break.'

Besides illegal crayfishing, he started stealing cars and us-ing false credit cards.

Dehumanizing Effect

According to his brother, Peter McCall, his wife 'may have been too demanding and put unnecessary pressures on him'. But, then, she had a lot to put up with.

McCall went back to gaol and his wife divorced him, al-though, as in the case of Stander and Bekkie, he remained fond of her.

He planned to use some of his loot from the bank hopping raids to provide for his child (now thirteen) and his ex-wife, even though she had remarried.

According to Peter McCall, gaol had a terrible impact on his brother 'the dehumanizing effect that he personally felt'. Leigh McCall did not hate society but, Peter McCall con-tinued, 'His view of society was coloured by the manner in which the rules of society were enforced by warders, those fairly mindless moronic kind of dispensers of incarceration. At no stage did he have a pathological vengeance on society as a whole.'

His brother described McCall as 'a loner, very self suffi-cient'.

'Allan Heyl is a non-entity, he is not a survivor. André and Leigh were both resourceful and could survive. It's unfortu-nate that they were caught.

'One of the things which is sad,' continued Peter McCall, 'is that he happened to get involved in what was going to become a very status conscious case in so far as the Police's pride was concerned.'

While he was on the run as a member of the Stander gang,

he took enormous risks. He regularly called up and even upon friends and relatives. He complained about loneliness. He played upon old ties, but often his friends were too scared to help him. His boyhood friends now had families and responsible jobs. The videos, callgirls, the excitement and fear of robbery were not enough; McCall still hankered for his past.

Perhaps his lengthy stay in hospital with a broken leg and jaw gave him time to brood on what had been.

Minimum Force

McCall's family was very disturbed by the manner of the police shootout. 'It transgresses the bounds of the principle of minimum force.' His family also criticised the Police for not informing them before the media.

But what of McCall's violence in the Randburg gun shop? The family believes that it was a case of mistaken identity; it was Heyl, not McCall. That is a natural family reaction. Like Stander, the families have rallied around.

McCall did not have a previous record of armed robbery: 'The use of violence – mechanical violence not personal strength – was certainly out of character,' said his brother.

Personality Clash

Did a personality clash spring up with Stander? McCall did tell his family about rifts in the gang. But he was not a meek follower of the gang leader. 'He was mutually using and being used by Stander.'

At McCall's funeral one hundred and thirty people attended. His brother said: 'He was highly regarded by his friends. If one actually looks at the number of people who came from vast distances to his funeral which was not advertised at all, only by word of mouth, when one compares that with André's which was a totally advertised affair.'

Leigh McCall could not tolerate authority. He was a born rebel, with no cause except his own. His brother spoke about Leigh's childhood problems, but 'at the end of the day, he was responsible for his own fate.'

A close friend of McCall's said he was not surprised at McCall's death. 'It was inevitable. I predicted it. He'd rather die than be caught.'

15

One That Got Away

Allan George Heyl
Age: Thirty two years
Height: one meter eight
Description: Has thin light brown hair and normally wears thick glasses with brown rims
Education: Hoërskool Hentie Cilliers in Virginia, matriculated, studied towards a teaching degree in Bloemfontein but dropped out in his final year
Marital Status: Divorced
Criminal Record
• Aged twenty one, he was first sent to gaol for three years after being convicted on five counts of robbery.
• He served only two years of his sentence and was released on parole in 1975.
• In 1977 he was again found guilty on five counts of armed robbery with aggravating circumstances and was sentenced to an effective period of fifteen years' imprisonment.

Heyl attended Hentie Cilliers Hoërskool in Virginia. A former school mate said of Heyl: 'He had as little interest in sport as he had in girls. He would rather read poetry then join the others smoking in the toilets.' He had a special flair for mathematics . . . a skill he passed on in classes at Zonderwater Prison. Perhaps, too, Heyl was the one who counted the money after the bank heists. Certainly he was there to advise Stander when it came to the big splurge on the yacht.

Ironically, one of Heyl's school chums, Dougie Scheepers, became equally notorious. Scheepers was sentenced to death in 1979 after being convicted of a spate of armed robberies with a sawn off shotgun in Johannesburg. The death penalty was later commuted to thirty years' imprisonment.

Heyl's mother describes him as a 'super boy'. During his school days he was never any trouble to her. He was known as an introverted type who made few friends of either sex. He often used to tell teachers and classmates that he would be very rich some day. But he opted for a profession which was hardly likely to bring him dramatic wealth – teaching. Then in his last year at Bloemfontein Teachers Training College, the promising student who had never been a problem to his parents dropped out.

All Divorced

Like Stander, Heyl had problems conforming to authority. Heyl was caught stealing while training to be a store manager at Woolworths in Cape Town. His wife divorced him. All three of the Stander gang were divorced men.

'I don't know what motivated him or made him change his mind about what he wanted out of life. When people grow up they make their own decisions,' said Heyl's mother, Mrs Rose Heyl.

A year after finishing his prison sentence he teamed up with Neville Cahi, a friend he had made in gaol. The two launched a four month bank robbery spree using toy pistols. Heyl pioneered the use of full face helmets as a method of disguise and powerful motorbikes for a fast getaway.

A woman who was close to Heyl said: 'It wasn't as though he needed the money. He seemed to have other reasons for doing it. He was never violent. Allan never hurt anyone and I can't understand why they say he is dangerous.'

Heyl went on a spending spree, buying a car, a motorcycle, a TV and a washing machine. Stander behaved much the same after his robberies, buying cars and indulging in luxurious trips to Mauritius.

When Heyl was caught he was given an effective eleven year gaol term. He had been in prison for three years when Stander arrived. They became friends. Heyl had quickly become an 'A' grade prisoner entitled to maximum privileges.

After years of planning, Stander and McCall broke out in August 1983. Two months later they freed Heyl while he was doing a trade test in Olifantsfontein on the East Rand.

Shortly after the raid on the Randburg gun shop, McCall broke a leg and his jaw in a motor car accident. So Heyl, previously only the driver, became a gunman side by side with Stander on the raids.

This should surprise no one as he was an experienced armed robber – hardly an apprentice.

In spite of the notoriety gained by Heyl, the family has stuck by him as have the Standers and McCalls, all defending their relatives' reputations.

Mrs Heyl, Allan's mother, said: 'I am very upset about what has happened and I am very worried about what will become of Allan, but I would never reject him just like that, I am his mother,' she said straightforwardly.

She was angry that newspaper reports had claimed that she no longer cared for her son or that she never wanted to see him again. 'He had a good upbringing and he was good at school. In spite of what some people have said, he was not an aggressive person.'

'I'm Sorry, Mom'

Mrs Heyl had never heard of André Stander until the gaol break. 'I have never seen Stander but I feel very sorry for his parents. I know what they must be going through,' she said. 'I don't know how Allan will make out on his own. I just wish I knew where he was. I know that if I saw him again he would say, "I'm sorry, Mom."'

Privately, the Heyl family is reconciled to the worst. But is Heyl dead? There is no hard evidence to suggest that André Stander betrayed any member of his gang. After the

177

McCall shootout, it is known that Heyl made a hasty exit from Johannesburg. The evidence of the dumping in Pretoria of a stolen motor car probably used by him suggests a rapid and unplanned shift in plans.

Was he the mystery voice to Tomasello in America? Were the American police using Tomasello as a classic Hollywood piece of bait to trap Heyl if he was in the United States? Or has he gone to ground in Britain?

Wherever he is, he has so far survived. Ironically, he was considered to be the 'softest' of the trio. In the end, he is the hardest, the brightest – or is he just the luckiest?

16

Don't Bank On It

Old robbers never die, they just steal away . . . or they get caught.

There was a hundred percent decrease in robberies on banks and building societies in the months following the break up of the Stander gang. For example, after a robbery on Nedbank on the 4th February 1984, for more than thirty days not a single bank or building society in Johannesburg was raided.

Banking may well be a career from which no man really recovers, but bank robbing was getting almost as risky. As of the beginning of March, the Police had solved almost sixty percent of the bank and building society robberies in the previous six months.

Stopping the Stander gang, which was involved in at least twenty seven robberies netting R532 268 in cash, mainly from financial institutions, played a major role in the crime downswing.

'Very hard work and determination,' according to Brigadier Manie van der Linde, head of the Brixton Murder and Robbery Squad, was behind the police success.

Of course the American police helped, as did increased security by the banks. Standard Bank has decided to spend millions more on one of the most sophisticated security systems in South Africa. The Bank has already installed steel bars in many of its branches, although, as Standard Bank spokesman, Bill Jones, said: 'The Standard Bank is dedicated primarily to the protection of its staff and secondly to the protection of its assets.'

The new security measures will include very expensive bullet proof glass.

Trust Bank has also stepped up its security. More hidden cameras are being utilised . . . the publicity given to the videos taken by Barclays of the Stander gang was a crucial element in their capture. More time locks, under counter devices controlling and delaying the release of money, will be installed. Another device is a cash dispenser which enables the cashier to withdraw only a limited amount of money. This forces the cashier to go to the main vault for big sums.

Successful Robberies

All these security factors will help to delay even the most determined thief. And security studies suggest that for a robbery to be successful it has to be completed within three minutes.

Undercover work has also played a part in stopping bank robbers. The South African Police has a very efficient network of informers.

Another deterrent is offering rewards. The official procedure is that the Police must recommend to the Clearing Bankers' Association of South Africa anyone whose tip has led to the arrest and conviction of someone plotting or executing a bank robbery.

During the hunt public excitement rose as the reward offered by the Clearing Bankers' Association started to tot up to astronomical figures.

The Press ran stories continually as the robberies mounted.

'Huge Price on Stander's Head,' ran one headline.

'Bank Rewards now over R220 000,' said another.

'*Reward!* R225 000 for bank hopper gang,' screamed another.

The Rand Daily Mail said: 'Colonel Fred Bull, the police public relations officer for the Witwatersrand, yesterday spelt out the conditions under which rewards would be given by the Clearing Bankers' Association, which represents most of South Africa's main banks.

'Colonel Bull said the R5 000 rewards offered applied to each individual bank robbery solved, and not to the total number of robberies committed by the suspect.

'In the bank hopping series, for instance, where the Stander gang is linked to at least sixteen robberies, the person who tips off the Police would be in line for R5 000 for each of the robberies committed.

'Should it be proved the Stander gang had in fact committed sixteen robberies, the informant could qualify for about R80 000.'

This particular report also went on to detail the circumstances whereby the R5 000 reward (per bank) could be doubled to R10 000. It would require the permission of two members of the Security Commission of the Clearing Bankers' Association, as well as a recommendation by a police officer of or above the rank of colonel.

The Citizen reported:

'After last weeks' daring armed robberies at three Johannesburg banks and one at Isando in which the "bank hoppers" netted more than R250 000, rewards offered by the Clearing Bankers' Association of South Africa have accumulated to a total of R225 000 for information leading to the arrest and conviction of the robbers.'

The *Sunday Tribune* was even more effusive: 'A staggering R225 000 of more in reward money has built up following a wave of fifteen lightning robberies which has stripped Witwatersrand banks of at least half a million rand within the last two months . . .

'The final tally of reward money will probably be higher with promises from the South African Police of a secret "but substantial" reward from their own coffers.

'Major Corrie Maree, of the Johannesburg Murder and Robbery Squad at Brixton, who is spearheading investigations, said the reward money being offered by the Clearing

Bankers' Association of South Africa was R5 000 for each person arrested and convicted on each count!'

However, when the time came for the dark suited geese of bankerdom to step into their vaulted nesting boxes to lay the golden reward eggs, then suddenly things had changed.

The Clearing Bankers' Association shook their collective heads and disclaimed all knowledge of there being an accumulative reward in respect of the bank hoppers.

They had never said it.

All they had said was there would be a R5 000 reward.

Just look at their notice!

It might, of course, even have to be split up between all deserving claimants.

They have pointed out, too, that the Police have made no recommendations to them yet as to whether anyone merits a reward.

Biting On The Golden Bullet

This smug attitude of the Bankers is hardly what one would expect for such an august body – or is it?

Public statements were made by the Press in their name, which if they were wrong, one would have expected them to publicly deny at the time. Instead they bit on the golden bullet (or whatever they bite on in financial circles) and said nothing.

The legal boys would call it misrepresentation by silence – so would a lot of other people.

But, one might ask, would any crook or informer, no matter how desperate, be likely to risk the wrath and vengeance of the underworld by grassing on a hard man like Stander for a lousy R5 000?

So far only two people have said they intend claiming the rewards offered for helping to capture the Stander gang: Peter Snyman, the owner of the Houghton shootout house, and Tony Tomasello.

17

Making of a Myth

Being a hero is about the shortest lived profession in the world. But did Stander's brief spate of infamy – or glory – really earn him the honour usually accorded a folk hero?

Stander hit the public spot in a way unknown since Scotty Smith or – a more striking parallel – the Foster gang which was active before the Great War. Like Stander, William Foster teamed up with two other hoods 'Maxim' Maxwell and 'Boy' Nezer.

While on the run for about a year, they robbed and killed several people, although there is doubt whether Foster himself ever killed anybody. Foster tried to live a respectable suburban life while on the run. He moved into a house in Regents Park, Johannesburg, along with his wife Peggy, and their baby. Eventually, they were cornered and hid out in a cave in Kensington. After parleying with the Police, the young baby was passed out of the cave. Then William and Peggy Foster committed suicide.

Foster became a legend. And so did Stander, but with apparently more public sympathy because he didn't kill anybody.

The frequently supportive public response says more about South African society than about Stander. As a sociologist at the University of the Witwatersrand said: 'When we come to lionize banditry in this way it indicates the Wild West values that have been bred into us over the years.

'We are a nation of cowboys, always ready to whip out our six shooters and start blasting away.'

But the Stander mania went deeper than just a trigger happy populace. As a psychiatrist explained: 'Haven't you ever wanted to rob a bank, get rich quick, drive a flamboyant yellow Porsche, be tough, strong and smart and thumb your nose at authority?

'Most South Africans are exposed to too much bureaucracy and control from the state in every aspect of their lives so they like to see someone get away with it when they revolt against the system.'

This viewpoint was taken a up by 'Amused Onlooker' from Johannesburg in a letter to the *Sunday Times:*

'But the reality is that, whatever his crimes, André Stander as he appears to the average person in our country (black and white alike), is something of a hero.

To many he is a cult figure. And irritating though this may be to the Police authorities, should those in power not contemplate the deeper meaning of this?

Many in our society, it seems, applaud virtually anyone who thumbs his nose at authority . . . especially a notorious and glamorous bank robber who makes lots of money, drives a Porsche Targa, goes to the best massage parlours and eats in the best restaurants.

In all this, I believe, there is a worrying message for our rulers, they should think deeply about the meaning of the hero status accorded Stander.

So Stander was the hero of the hour. He grabbed all the things that people liked. But then he was killed. Maybe that satisfied the public need as well, not just the voyeurism of seeing his body on TV but his punishment satisfied many people who admired his lifestyle. They want the Porsche *et al,* but they could never really get it. 'Stander did. Good for him, but he must not be allowed to get away with it, because neither can I.' Jealousy and *Schadenfreude* is probably stronger than public morality.

Another factor which evoked popular sympathy was Stander's (inaccurate) image that he attacked banks not helpless individuals. Banks are frequently regarded as impersonal, unresponsive – even rude – queue ridden institutions. Hence the welcome accorded to autobanks: they're a lot more friendly than most human tellers. For this reason his crimes were sometimes viewed as somewhat less reprehensible.

Romantic Rebel

Stander was also portrayed as a romantic rebel who didn't harm anybody. In this Stander was similar to the jewel thief, Sean Collins, alias Raffles. During the early 1970s he was dubbed the 'gentle crook' and it was said that his biggest fear was that he would injure someone if he was disturbed in the middle of a robbery. He even wrote to newspapers thanking them for their sympathetic portrayal of him.

Of course, a major element in Stander's hagiography was his saint-sinner, cop-crook persona. As one Stander observer put it: 'He has illustrated a thin line between cops and robbers. People like to see authority blundering in public.'

Ferdi van den Bergh, who was a friend of Stander's at Zonderwater Prison, says that Stander had told him that he robbed banks 'for the fun of it'. He was also 'motivated by a desire to take a swipe at society'.

Van den Bergh's views are supported by Cor van Deventer. He said: 'All his actions after prison were pointed towards *'Ek sal hulle wys* - I'll show them.' But his vengefulness, according to Cor van Deventer, was specifically aimed at the South African Police.

Did Stander really damage the South African Police? An officer involved in the hunt for Stander said: 'I hope not. We prosecuted him in the first place. We didn't pack him off to Switzerland. And what really annoys me is that he was a criminal, not a rogue policeman. He had ceased being a policeman.'

A High Class Bandit

'Back in the old days,' recalled Van Deventer, 'when we used to go to the Wild Coast on holiday together, we often used to fantasise about what we wanted most in life. I wanted a small holding and a horse for the kids but he wanted the high life. I think he planned to sail that boat he bought.'

Stander was the high class bandit in South Africa. He did not skulk in a cheap Hillbrow hotel, sweating over every phone call, twitching at every knock of the door, peering out at the world through grimy curtains. No, it was beautiful women, a flashy yellow Porsche, a superb yacht and flamboyant behaviour. Even in his straightened circumstances in America he still acted out the playboy role.

He had personal style, but was he a stylish crook? Men who were in the Police with Stander have criticised the description of him as a 'brilliant' cop. As a detective, ex-colleague Chris Swanepoel, said earlier: 'He couldn't even catch a cold.'

An officer involved in the Cape Town hunt for Stander said that Stander was 'a bad armed robber'. 'There is a chap called Richard Loewenstein. He single handedly got a half a million rand. He also left the country.'

Loewenstein, a charming Jewish crook dubbed the 'Saville Row Robber', specialised in jewellery thefts. He would steal a car such as a Porsche by switching seats and leaving the salesman standing. Then he would ring up a top jeweller and arrange for the best stock to be ready for him, as he said he was busy. Then he would walk off with the loot. A playboy life style, the best cars, impeccable manners, he even wrote the Cape Town police a letter apologising for the inconvenience he caused them. This thirty five year old 'gentleman' robber did it alone and got away with it; a Pink Panther who won. And he had far more panache than Stander.

But the Cape Town officer did agree that there were some points he would concede to Stander. 'I admire him for nothing else except that he had incredibly good taste when it came to buying the yacht.'

He also recognised another important aspect of Stander's *modus operandi*. 'Where Stander did very well is that he realised that people in your more affluent suburbs look less into their neighbours back yards than people in poorer suburbs. Something he had learned when a former policeman.

'I can tell you stories of housebreakings in affluent suburbs where the chaps would rock up in a big delivery van and drive away with all the furniture and the neighbours wouldn't know. In the more affluent suburbs people have never bothered to pass the time of day with their neighbours. He was clever in that.'

If he was that bad, why did it take the South African Police so long to get him?

The Cape Town policeman paused and said: 'Okay, it took us a damn long time to find Stander.'

But weren't the American police much more on the ball?

The officer demurred: 'The Yanks weren't all that hot. We gave them the addresses.'

Series of Blunders

In America Stander made a series of blunders which led to his death.

As Van Deventer put it: 'I can't understand what happened to him towards the end. Perhaps he was frightened by McCall's death. Maybe he started cracking up.

'Maybe the crack up started when he began to need others to come along with him on jobs that he at first pulled alone. First, he needed one back up then two. Maybe he was already scared, already losing confidence.'

But even before the last days in America, the one time policeman ignored or forgot the techniques he had learned while in the Force. A big mistake was to leave his partner McCall with a written address in Fort Lauderdale which the Police were to find in the Houghton house after the shootout. Stander should have made McCall memorize the address, which was a key element in the plan to leave the Republic.

But by that time Stander had been free for more than five

months and had pulled a string of successful bank jobs. The possibility that he or one of his lieutenants could ever be caught was probably ignored or pushed into his sub conscious. A seemingly unimportant detail concerning the Fort Lauderdale address was no doubt forgotten.

And it was a big risk to use girls from escort agencies.

Sure, Stander was popular, and high class prostitutes operating from the disreputable agencies would have no particular affection for the Police. But, considering the award money and the loose talk on the periphery of the underworld, the chances of a leak were high.

Carelessness and arrogance were the crucial factors which eventually cost Stander his life. So, despite his love of cops and robber movies, Stander finished as a victim, not the hero of a real life drama.

Executioner's Song

Perhaps Stander wanted it that way. Cor van Deventer said that Stander read Norman Mailer's *The Executioner's Song* about Gary Gilmore's fight to be allowed to be executed. Stander also hired the video when he was on the run.

'In it there is a description,' said Van Deventer, 'of a criminal's last moments, and Stander re-enacted them for me. Afterwards he spoke in English – the language he always used when he wanted to be dramatic – and told me about his feelings about death.'

According to Van Deventer, Stander admitted that the 'ultimate pleasure left to me now is death'.

Freud maintained that the death instinct is more basic than the life preserving impulses of self preservation and sexuality. Such a death wish is not necessarily a suicidal tendency since individuals with a self destructive drive can be very aggressive in their own defence. Some of Stander's life, particularly his relations with an authoritarian father figure, fit exact descriptions of classical studies of death wishes. The impact of his brother's violent death also matches the classic psychoanalytical studies.

Freud used the name of the Greek personification of death, Thanatos, to represent the death wish. A person with a death wish can still exhibit a great zest for life, even the high life. So Stander could wish for the yacht, but then put himself in a dangerous position over and over again. A characteristic aspect of a death wish is to keep repeating things that are dangerous or frightening.

Will Rogers, the American humorist, once wrote: 'This thing of being a hero, about the main thing to it is to know when to die.'

One psychological explanation of the childish mistakes made by Stander in his last days is not that he was cracking but that sub-consciously he had decided to die.

A Cape Town psychiatrist, who has specialised in criminal cases, said that the rogue former cop seemed to have had, 'a personality disorder with psychopathic traits'.

'He wasn't a psychopath at heart. He was wanting to be caught . . . he set himself up to be caught.'

The psychiatrist further suggested that André Stander was rebelling against his father's 'authoritarian expectations'. The medical expert speculated on why Stander had become a folk hero: 'Because there was no political way of bucking the system, to many blacks and whites Stander was popular because he was anti authority, even if he was fighting with criminal and not with political intent.'

What Is Left?

So what is left of the Stander myth?

His image has been that of the romantic rebel, a subject of envy for his speedy canary yellow (even though stolen) Porsche Targa and his ocean going yacht (even though the Police made sure it didn't go anywhere).

But as *Beeld* succinctly said: *'iets het skeef geloop'* - something went wrong.

Until Heyl is caught, the name will remain in the headlines. But perhaps Heyl will vanish like Lord Lucan who is still wanted by Scotland Yard for murder.

Sick jokes about Stander and Stander types became the instant rage. *Wits Wits,* the rag mag of the University of the Witwatersrand, satirised the Stander gang: 'Robbing banks is a great way to get rich (try hitting them towards the end of the month), chic (you can live in Houghton) and progressive (if you give your money to poor yacht owners).' Wits rag stuntmen also 'borrowed' the Porsche used by Stander from a Springs garage, and later posed as his gang to raise money for charity.

The spate of books, films, songs and even T-shirts on Stander will rework and reinvigorate the myth. They are more likely to enhance the legend, not debunk Stander . . . quite simply, people like to have heroes.

Cor van Deventer said of his former friend's popular canonisation: 'He wanted to be the Number One criminal. He's becoming a folk hero; he'll be very happy wherever he is.'

Did Van Deventer consider Stander a hero?

'I can't understand that. I can't understand how the hell people can consider him a hero at all. I don't think men can point guns at ladies, take money from them and consider themselves heroes. The moment you hold a firearm at somebody, what else is that but a death threat, never matter how soft you speak and what good things you say to her. You can even tell her you love her and hold a damn gun to her and that's a life threat.

'It would have been a different matter if he had walked unarmed into a bank and then in a heroic way somehow got the money from men. Then I would say the guy was a hero. He was no Robin Hood robbing the rich to feed the poor. With him charity began at home.

'The basis of the legend is that he never killed anybody, but that doesn't mean he never shot anybody.'

Even though Stander was not a murderer, he would likely have gone to the gallows for his crimes. He was an habitual and dangerous criminal, not a hero.

Not all the public response polished Stander's halo. 'Vigilante' in the *Sunday Times* wrote:

I find the glamorization of André Stander to be both sickening and outrageous: people and their emotions are perfidious.

Really . . . the man was nothing more than a villain who robbed other people's money for his own enrichment.

He committed crime after crime at the point of a gun

and on more than one occasion could have killed.

Although in the minority, other letters to the Press supported the much harangued South African Police:
He Was A Traitor, Not A Hero

It is wrong to think that there was something smart in the exploits of the gangster, André Stander.

A police officer who turns to crime betrays his trust, and is a traitor to his country.

Let us reserve our admiration for all those of the South African Police who are true to their trust.

If we take the side of Stander, we are setting the worst possible example to the youth of this country.
Justice, Johannesburg

One letter to the *Rand Daily Mail* took the unusual angle of blaming the banks for encouraging the Stander gang:
Banks Invite People Like Stander & Co

. . . I would like to point out that the blame for these outrageous crimes should be placed squarely on the shoulders of the financial institutions.

It is not for the lack of police surveillance, but rather the inadequate security procedures adopted by these institutions.

In contrast to South Africa, most banks abroad have either armed guards at each entrance and/or bullet proof partitions between teller and the general public.

Apparently the banks in this country view this system of security detrimental to their 'personal bank/client relationship' image.

Furthermore, I doubt whether our police force has the time or manpower to guard every bank, building society and one person operated (normally a female) building society agencies to combat these escalating felonies.

. . . Financial institutions should stop turning their operations into potential film scripts for 'stars' like Stander and Company.
B Rational, Bloemfontein

An Enduring Myth

Time and T-shirts will do no harm to the Stander myth. After all, Jesse James shot children, but only in fact, not in folklore. Stander the robber did not kill or want to kill anybody in the myth, although he did shoot or be associated with shootings at people, one of them a woman, on at least two occasions.

Stander had cheek, and a lot of luck. He was not a successful armed robber because he got caught in the end but his audacity charmed and caught the imagination of a bored public. As the officer in charge of the Cape Town hunt for Stander put it: 'All I can say is that people must have incredibly dull lives if this could really excite them.'

As you get older, it is harder to have heroes, but to many people they are necessary. The opportunities for heroism in ordinary life are very limited: the most people can do is sometimes not to be as weak as they've been at other times. Perhaps, in terms of his psyche, Stander had always been a weak, obsessed man. In his career of crime, he worked out his obsessions and contradictions feverishly; he found a new strength but a strength that had to be by definition short lived.

So he became the jet setting hero he had always wanted to be. But by robbing banks so audaciously the hero's almost inevitable fate was descend rapidly from hero to zero. If the psychiatrist is right, he wanted to get caught.

He had to be caught for the sake of the heroic legend that was building up about him.

'Show me a hero,' said F Scott Fitzgerald, 'and I will write you a tragedy.'

The public loves a tragedy, more than a good luck story, even if they say that they are sorry that Stander was dealt his comeuppance so violently. By lionizing him, South African society played the game the way André Stander wanted. So even in death he won.

Unhappy is any society that needs such a hero.